The Court Rolls
of the
Honor of Clitheroe
1568 – 1571

Helmshore Local History
2(

ISBN 0 906881 09 9

British Library Cataloguing in Publication Data. A catalogue record for this book is available from the British Library.

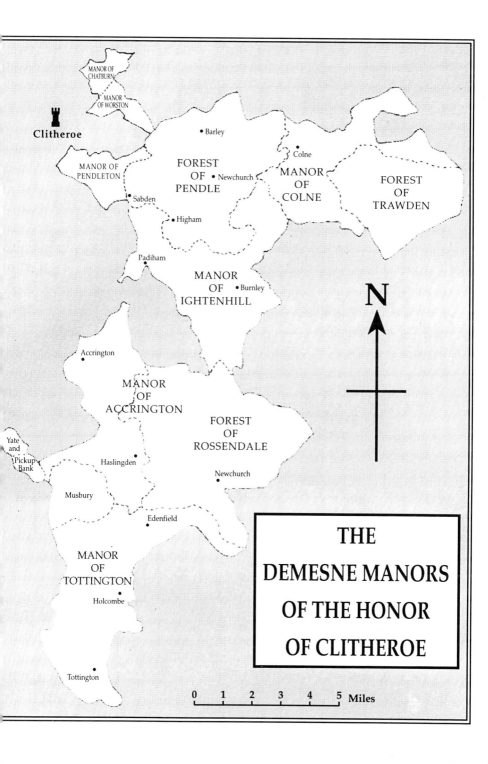

MANOR OF
CHATBURN

MANOR
OF WORSTON

Clitheroe

MANOR OF
PENDLETON

• Barley

FOREST
OF
PENDLE

• Newchurch

Colne

MANOR
OF
COLNE

FOREST
OF
TRAWDEN

• Sabden

• Higham

Padiham

MANOR
OF
IGHTENHILL

• Burnley

N

Accrington

MANOR
OF
ACCRINGTON

FOREST
OF
ROSSENDALE

Yate
and
Pickup
Bank

Haslingden

Newchurch

Musbury

Edenfield

MANOR
OF
TOTTINGTON

Holcombe

Tottington

THE
DEMESNE MANORS
OF THE HONOR
OF CLITHEROE

0   1   2   3   4   5 Miles

INTRODUCTION

This book is the second in the series of transcriptions of the court rolls of the Honor of Clitheroe to be published by Helmshore Local History Society. The three rolls it covers are deposited at the Lancashire Record Office under reference DDHCL 3/51, 3/52 and 3/53. They are published with the kind permission of the Hon. R.C. Assheton, Lord of the Honor. Thanks are also due to Mr. Bruce Jackson, the County Archivist; Mr. Thomas Woodcock, Norroy and Ulster King of Arms; and Dr. Peter Franklin. The book has been produced with the financial assistance of the Marc Fitch Fund, which is gratefully acknowledged.

For information on the Honor of Clitheroe, the rolls and the operation of the halmote courts, readers are referred to the introduction to *The Court Roll of the Honor of Clitheroe 1567 – 1568.*

EDITORIAL POLICY

The text that follows is not a word for word transcription and translation of the original. Many legal phrases are repeated again and again in the rolls, but add nothing to our knowledge of the people and places of Tudor Lancashire. We have, therefore, followed William Farrer's example of providing what amounts to a summary of all relevant information contained in the entries on the rolls. The end result is nearer to the original than Farrer's work since, for example, he did not always list the names of the manorial jury or give details of the pleas heard by the courts.

The original spellings of any place-names, surnames and other proper names have been retained. The spelling of passages in English in the rolls has been modernised, except for occasional words that are given in single inverted commas: 'laithez'. The use of capitals and punctuation have been modernised throughout.

Where a Latin word or phrase is given with its English translation, it appears in square brackets thus: [*'vagantes'*]. Uncertain readings are indicated by [*?*] and illegible words by a series of full stops, the number of stops being approximately the same as the number of illegible letters. Editorial comments are given in square brackets.

Figures in Roman numerals in the original have been given in Arabic figures in the transcript. For example, 3s 4d for iiis ivd. Where a figure appears above a name in the rolls, it is given in brackets after the name in the transcript.

An ultra-violet light source has been used to recover as much of the text as possible in places where the rolls are worn or damaged.

Readers wishing to compare the wording of the transcript with the wording of the original rolls should consult the introduction to *The Court Roll of the Honor of Clitheroe 1567 – 1568* where a number of examples of entries are given transcribed and translated word for word.

GLOSSARY

AFFEEROR	–	Officer appointed to fix the amount of an amercement.
AGISTMENT	–	A right to summer grazing.
AMERCEMENT	–	A fine for some misdemeanour. Not to be confused with an entry fine (*q.v.*).
APPRAISER	–	Officer appointed to estimate the value of property.
ASSIGN	–	One to whom property or rights were legally transferred.
BAILIFF	–	An official in charge of two or three manors. Above the greave, but subordinate to the steward.
BOVATE	–	*see* Oxgang.
CAPITAL MESSUAGE	–	A large house.
DEMESNE	–	Strictly speaking demesne was property held directly from the Lord of the Manor, but in the Honor of Clitheroe the word is often applied to the main farm or house of a large estate. For example, Lumb Hall, near Edenfield was the demesne of the estate belonging to the Rawstorne family.
DISSEISED	–	*see* Seised.
DOWER	–	A portion of an estate (usually one third) claimed by a widow in her lifetime or until she remarried.
ENFEOFFMENT	–	Legally putting some one in possession of property.
ENTRY FINE	–	Payment made when some one was formally admitted to a property. Equivalent to one year's customary rent.
FENCE LOOKER	–	Officer appointed to supervise the good repair of fences or walls and enclosures.
FEOFFEE (OF TRUST)	–	A trustee.
GREAVE	–	Also known as a reeve. The chief officer of the manor elected by the manorial tenants. He was mainly responsible for the collection of rents and taxes.
HALMOTE	–	The court of the Lord of the Manor.
JOINTURE	–	The holding of property to the joint use of a husband and wife as a provision for the latter during her widowhood.

MESSUAGE	–	A house, its outbuildings and yard.
MOSS	–	An area of peat where turfs could be cut. *See also* Turbary.
OXGANG	–	A variable measure of land related to the amount an ox could plough in a year. Also known as a bovate.
POUNDER	–	Official in charge of the pound or pinfold into which stray animals were driven and released only on payment of a fine.
QUITCLAIM	–	A release and disclaimer of all rights, interest and potential legal actions from grantor to grantee.
RELEASE	–	The act of conveying or making over property or rights to another; a deed or document for this purpose.
REMAINDER	–	The residual interest from a legal estate, created by the same conveyance by which the estate itself was granted.
REMISE	–	To give up, surrender or make over to another.
RESCUE	–	The forcible taking of a person or goods out of legal custody; forcible recovery (by the owner) of goods distrained.
REVERSION	–	A future interest in a piece of property.
RODELAND (RODLAND)	–	Land which had been 'ridded' or cleared from the waste.
SEISED	–	An individual who owned property was said to be 'seised' of it. If dispossessed, he was 'disseised'.
SELION	–	The basic unit of cultivation in an open field, usually consisting of a ridge with furrows either side.
SUIT (To do)	–	To appear at the manorial court.
SUIT OF MILL/ SOKE OF MILL	–	The manorial tenant's obligation to grind his corn at the Lord of the Manor's mill and payment for the same.
TOFT	–	The site of a house and its outbuildings; a homestead.
TURBARY	–	The right to cut peat for fuel on the commons.
VILL	–	A settlement.

COURT ROLL OF THE HONOR OF CLITHEROE
MICHAELMAS 1568 - EASTER 1569

Halmote of the manors of Chatburne, Worston and Penhulton held at Clitherowe Castle, Monday, 6th December, 11 Elizabeth I [1568] before John Towneley, chief steward there.

Inquisition taken there for the Queen to make enquiry upon the oaths of Roger Nowell, gent., Thomas Robinson, Thomas Tailior, William Smythez, John Dugdale, senior, Thomas Ryley, John Dugdale, junior, Edmund Dawson, Ottiwell Feilden, John Wulton, James Alth'm, Geoffrey Kendall, Nicholas Blakey, and John Dawson.

Chatburne
Thomas Nowell was elected greave of Wurston [*sic*]; Henry Lund and Thomas Ballde were elected constables of Chatburne.

William Tailior (20d) because he drew blood from Nicholas Blakey.
Amercements 20d.

Wurston
Richard Grenacars, gent., was elected both greave and constable of Wurston.

Henry Migecocke (4d) because he enclosed a parcel of the highway in Wurston.
Amercements 4d.

Penhulton
Thomas Shuttlewurth was elected greave of Penhulton; William Sydgreves and John Wolton were elected constables of Penhulton.

Penhulton
One messuage, other buildings, one garden and 20 acres of oxgang land in Penhulton came into the Queen's hands at about the time of the last court by the death of Anthony Watson, gent. Thomas Watson was his son and next heir and was of full age. Admittance sought and granted. Fine 6s 8d by the pledge of John More.

Sum of this halmote 8s 3d approved.

Halmote of the manors of Chatburne, Wurston and Penhulton held at Clitherowe Castle, Monday, 18th July, 11 Elizabeth I [1569] before John Towneley, esq., chief steward there.

Inquisition taken there for the Queen to make enquiry upon the oaths of Thomas Robinson, Richard Kendall, senior, Thomas Tailior, William Smithez, John Hird, John Harryson, Edmund Dawson, John Atkinson, John Dawson, Geoffrey Kendall,

Richard Dugdale, Christopher Migecock, Ottiwell Feilden, Francis Webster and John Moore.

Chatburne

John Tailior, senior, (2d) because he kept his pigs on the common pasture in Chatburne called le Cowe pasture contrary to the bye-laws.

William Tailior (2d) for the same offence.

Margaret Bollds (2d) and Thomas Bolld (2d) because they kept their fences called le ringe[?] yarde open, to the damage of their neighbours.

Agnes, lately wife of Thomas Kendall, deceased, (12d) because her servants broke the Queen's fold or pound.

Richard Dugdall (2d), the late wife of John Harr.pp (2d), John Ellill (2d), John Dugdale, junior, (2d) and James Harropp (2d) because they kept their pigs upon le Cowe pasture aforesaid contrary to the bye-laws.

Amercements 2s 6d.

Wurston

Richard Grenacars, gent., greave of Wurston, surrendered 3 acres of land within the vill of Wurston, now or lately in the tenure of Richard Dugdale, which the said Richard Dugdale delivered to him, to the use of Thomas Woode and Henry Wood and their heirs as feofees according to the intent. Admittance sought and granted. Fine 12d by the pledge of James Harropp.

The intent was that the feofees were to be seised of the property to the use of the said Richard Dugdale and Emma, his wife, for life and after their deaths to the use of John Dugdale, Richard's son, and his heirs for ever.

Sum of this halmote 3s 6d approved.

Sum total of the two aforesaid halmotes 11s 10d.
Penhulton 6s 8d total of fines for land; Chatburn 4s 2d total of amercements;
Wurston 12d total of fines for land.
Approved and charged in the 11th year of Queen Elizabeth.

Halmote of the manor of Ightenhill held at Higham, Tuesday, 7th December, 11 Elizabeth I [1568] before John Towneley, chief steward there.

Inquisition taken there for the Queen to make enquiry upon the oaths of John Robinson of Golldshaie, Edmund Robinson, senior, Lawrence Stevenson, James Robinson of Bareley, Richard Harteley, Christopher Hartley, Nicholas Robinson alias Thirneholme, Christopher Bawdwen, senior, Henry Hargreaves, Bernard Sutcliff, Ellis Nutter, George Cronckeshaie, son of Robert, Leonard Cronckeshaie, Edward Hargreaves and John Mitton.

Edmund Towneley, gent., was elected greave of Penhull.

One messuage, other buildings and certain lands, tenements, meadows, grazing lands and pastures in Whitleyeboithe in the Forest of Penhull, annual rent to the Queen 9s 3¼d, came into the Queen's hands by the death of James Hargreaves. Geoffrey Hargreaves was his son and next heir and was of full age. Admittance sought and granted. Double the aforesaid rent after the death of each tenant.[1] Fine 9s 3¼d by the pledge of John Hartley.

Richard Nutter, junior, surrendered by John Nutter of Neweland, a tenant of the Queen, one parcel of land and a certain parcel of one barn built upon the said parcel of land in Golldshaieboth in the Forest of Pendle, annual rent to the Queen 1d, and now or lately in the tenure of John Nutter, clerk. And also sufficient turbary for burning in one house in Golldshaieboith to the use of the said John Nutter, clerk, and his assigns from 15th April next after the date of this halmote for twenty years. John Nutter sought admittance by the said John Nutter of Neweland, his attorney, and it was granted. An annual rent of 3d was payable to Richard Nutter and his heirs at the usual feasts. Fine 1d by the pledge of the said John Nutter of Newelaund.

Leonard Cronckeshaie surrendered by Thomas Ryley, a tenant of the Queen, one messuage, other buildings and 4 acres of land, meadow, grazing land and pasture, now or lately in the tenure of Robert Emote, in le Westeclose in the Forest of Penhull, annual rent to the Queen 2d, to the use of the said Robert Emott and his assigns according to the intent. Admittance sought and granted. Fine 2d by the pledge of John Hargreaves of Barrowford.

[Membrane 1d]

The intent was that Robert Emot and his assigns were to be seised of the property, after the end of the title and interest which one Richard Bancrofte and his assigns had in it, to the use of the said Robert and his assigns for the life of the said Leonard Cronckeshaie. The said Robert and his assigns were to pay yearly to the said Leonard or his assigns the rent of 14s at Easter and Michaelmas or within ten days after either of the said feasts.

Richard Claye of Norland, gent., and Margaret, his wife, surrendered by Barnard Blakey, gent., (Margaret was examined and confessed alone by the steward and said she was not compelled but acted from her own free will)[2] the third part of one messuage, other buildings, lands, tenements, meadows, grazing lands and pastures with mosses in Rougheleigh in the Forest of Penhull, annual rent to the Queen 7s 4½d and the ninth part of ½d, to the use of Nicholas Whitacar of Highhill and Henry Blakey of Lower Barrowford and their assigns for ten years from 15th

---

[1] This clause giving details of when twice the customary rent was to be paid appears in each surrender of property that was in one of the Forests. It has been omitted from the remainder of this transcript.

[2] This clause appears whenever a woman joined her husband in making a surrender. It has been omitted from the remainder of this transcript.

April 1570. Admittance sought. Henry Harteley forbade fine for the dower of Agnes, his daughter. Nicholas Whitacar and Henry Blakey found pledges Barnard Blakey and John Mitton to answer the forbid. Admittance was then granted. Fine 7s 4½d and the ninth part of ½d by the pledges aforesaid.

Sum of this halmote 16s 10½d ¼d approved.

Penhull
Halmote of the manor of Ightenhill held at Higha', Thursday, 16th June, 11 Elizabeth I [1569] before John Towneley, esq., chief steward there.

Inquisition taken there for the Queen to make enquiry upon the oaths of John Harteley of Admergill, John Smyth, Christopher Smyth, Nicholas Robinson, junior, Christopher Bawdwen, junior, Henry Robinson, Thomas Verley, John Hartley of Bareley, John Mankenholes, Richard Nutter, Edmund Stevenson, John Baley, James Hargreaves of Dene, William Hargreaves, Richard Croke and Robert Jackson.

The jury said that they had nothing to present because all was peaceful, right and well.

Nicholas Robinson, greave of Penhull, surrendered one barn and one close and a parcel of arable land and meadow called le Horestones, containing 10 acres, in le Fence in the Forest of Pendle, annual rent to the Queen 3s 4d, and now or lately in the tenure of John Eastewood alias Nutter, to the use of Henry Robinson, son of the said John [sic], Barnerd, son of Barnard Parker of Alkencotz, John, son of Thomas Robinson, and Barnard Harteley of Lawnd, their heirs and assigns, as feofees according to an indenture dated 20th August 9 Elizabeth I [1567]. Admittance sought and granted. Fine 3s 4d by the pledge of John Hargreaves.

John Parker of Brownebrincks surrendered by John Nutter of Penhul, a tenant of the Queen, one messuage and other buildings, lands, meadows, grazing lands, and pastures in le Fence in the Forest of Penhull called le Brownebrincks, annual rent to the Queen 20s, now in the tenure of the said John Parker, to the use of John Nutter, John Harteley of Adm'gill, Edmund Parker and Henry Bawdwen and their heirs as feofees according to the intent. Admittance sought and granted. Fine 20s by the pledge of Hugh More.

The intent was that the feofees were to be seised of the property to the use of the said John Parker for life and after his death to the use and intent declared by the said John Parker in his last will and testament.

Alice, lately wife of John Nutter of Golldshaie, deceased, and now wife of Lawrence Butterfelde, and the said Lawrence, surrendered by Richard Smithez, in place of John Towneley, esq., chief steward there, all their part and portion which they had or may have had in future of any right of and in all messuages, other buildings, lands, tenements, meadows, grazing lands, pastures, moors and mosses of which the said John Nutter was seised for his lifetime by the right of Alice's dower in the Forest of Pehull [*sic*], annual rent to the Queen 1d, to the use of John Nutter, clerk, rector of the rectory of Sefton, and his assigns, for Alice's life. Admittance sought and granted. Fine 1d by the pledge of John Nutter of Newland.

Agnes, lately wife of Richard Nutter of Golldshaie, deceased, surrendered by Richard Smithez, deputy steward there, all her part and portion which she had or may have had in future of and in all messuages, other buildings, lands, tenements, meadows, grazing lands, pastures, moors and mosses in the Forest of Pendle, of which the said Richard was seised for his lifetime by right of Agnes's dower, annual rent to the Queen 4d, to the use of John Nutter, clerk, rector of the rectory of Sefton, and his assigns, for Agnes's life. Admittance sought and granted. Fine 4d by the pledge of John Nutter of Newelaund.

Christopher, son of Lawrence Harteley, surrendered one parcel of land called Humfray doole, being a parcel of Russheton thornes, in the Forest of Penhull, annual rent to the Queen 2s 1½d, and now or lately in the tenure of Alice Harteley, widow, which Christopher, son of Humphrey Harteley, and Barnard Hartley delivered to him, to the use of the said Alice and her assigns for thirteen years from the feast of the Invention of the Holy Cross last [May 3rd]. Admittance sought and granted. Fine 2s 1½d by the pledge of John Hargreaves.

[Membrane 2]

John Hartley of Adm'gill, William, son of James Hargreaves, and Hugh, son of Richard More, at the request of Hugh Moore of Highamdene, surrendered by John Nutter of Pendle, a tenant of the Queen, the fourth part of one close or parcel of land in le Fence in the Forest of Pendle called le Adlock Pasture, annual rent to the Queen 8d, and now or lately in the tenure of Nicholas Shore, to the said Nicholas and his assigns for life from 5th April last before the date of this court. Admittance sought and granted. Annual rent to the said Hugh More and his heirs 7s. Fine 8d by the pledge of John Nutter.

Robert Jackson of Redyehallows surrendered by Richard Woodroff, a tenant of the Queen, one messuage and other buildings and certain lands and tenements, meadows, grazing lands, pastures and mosses in Redyhallows in the Forest of Pendle, annual rent to the Queen 18s 6d [*The word* septodecem *has been altered to* octodecem], to Nicholas, son and heir of Geoffrey Russheton, gent., and Richard, son and heir of Hugh Hallstead, and their heirs as feofees according to indentures made by (1) the said Robert Jackeson and (2) Nicholas Hallstead of Padiham dated 9th February 8 Elizabeth I [1565/6]. Admittance sought and granted. Fine 18s 6d by the pledge of Lawrence Willson.

John Hancock of Lower Higham, son and heir apparent of Nicholas Hancock, gent., surrendered by Robert Cronckshey, a tenant of the Queen, one close of meadow called le Further Hey in Highamboth in the Forest of Pendle, annual rent to the Queen 6d, to the use of Thomas, son and heir apparent of Thomas Ryley, and John, son and heir apparent of Richard Croke of Westclose, and their assigns as feofees according to the intent. Admittance sought and granted. Fine 12d by the pledge of John Nutter.

The intent was that the feofees were to be seised of the close of land to the use of the said John Hancocke and Elizabeth, his wife, for their lives, and after their deaths to the use of the right heirs of the said John for ever.

Nicholas Robinson, greave of Penhull, surrendered one parcel of land called Croftend lying in Rugheleigh in the Forest of Penhull, annual rent to the Queen 6d, and now or lately in the tenure of Nicholas Robinson, junior, which the said Nicholas Robynson, junior, delivered to him, to William Harteley and his assigns for three years immediately after the end of thirteen years beginning at the feast of the Holy Cross [3rd May] which was in the ninth year of Queen Elizabeth [1567]. Admittance sought and granted. Fine 6d by the pledge of John Mytton.

Sum of this halmote 46s 6½d approved.

Sum total of the said two halmotes of Penhull
63s 5¼d total of fines for land.
Approved and charged in the 11th year of Queen Elizabeth.

Accrington
Halmote of the manor of Accryngton held there Monday, 13th December, 11 Elizabeth I [1568] before John Towneley, esq., chief steward there.

Inquisition taken there for the Queen to make enquiry upon the oaths of Francis Garsyde, gent., John Kenyon, Thomas Ryley, Robert Dureden, Richard Dureden, Robert Gregory, Henry Heap, James Roithewell, John Mankenholes, Robert Lange, Oliver Romesbothome, Giles Whitacar, John Ormerod, John Rydinge, Robert Ryley, senior, and Henry Ryleye.

Ralph Hollden, esq., was elected greave of Haslingden and Adam Hollden was admitted deputy greave; the said Ralph Hollden, esq., was elected constable of Haslingden and Ralph Talior was appointed deputy constable; Richard Dureden and Richard Hargreaves were elected fence lookers in Haslingden; Thomas Garsyed and Robert Gregory were elected appraisers for the Queen.

Haslingden
Edmund Romesbothome (12d) and William Barker (12d) because they made an affray together. Christopher Romesbothe' (3s 4d) because he kept illegal games, viz 'globes' in his tenement.

Amercements 5s 4d.

Thomas Ryley was elected greave of Accringeton Old Hold; James Yate was elected constable of Accrington; Giles Whitacar and Lawrence Jackeson were elected fence lookers.

Haslingden

Adam Hollden, greave of Haslingden, surrendered one acre of land in the north part of Kingsclough in Haslingden which Hugh Birtwisill, chaplain or clerk, delivered to him, to Henry Birtwisil, brother of the said Hugh, his heirs and assigns for ever. Admittance sought and granted. Fine 4d by the pledge of the said Adam Hollden.

Accrington Old Hold

John Kenyon surrendered by Richard Smythez, in place of John Towneley, esq., chief steward there, one barn and 28 acres of land in Mylneshawe enclosed with metes and bounds, to Christopher Kenyon, his son, and Anne, wife of the said Christopher, and their assigns, for life and after their deaths to the heirs of the said Christopher for ever. Admittance sought and granted. Fine 9s 4d by the pledge of Christopher Nuttowe.

William Ryley of Hawkeshay surrendered by John Kenyon and Robert Ryley, tenants of the Queen, one barn and 68 acres of land in Fearnyhaulgh in Accrington Old Hold, to Thomas Ryley, son and heir apparent of the said William, and his heirs for ever. Admittance sought. William forbade fine as he had all of the premises for life. The same was granted in open court and Thomas was then admitted. Fine 22s 8d by the pledge of Gilbert Russheton.

[Membrane 2d]

William Ryley of Hawkeshaie surrendered by John Kenyon and Robert Ryley, tenants of the Queen, one messuage, other buildings and 8 acres of land called le Brokilhurste in Accrington Old Hold, now or lately in the tenure of John Ryley, to the said John Ryley, his heirs and assigns, for ever. Admittance sought and granted. Fine 2s 8d by the pledge of Lawrence Nuttowe.

John Ryleie of Hawkeshaie surrendered by John Kenyon and Robert Ryleie, tenants of the Queen, 5 acres 3 roods of land in Hawkeshaie in Accrington Old Hold called le marled earth in Henfeild, to Thomas Ryley, his heirs and assigns for ever. Admittance sought. William Ryley, father of the said Thomas, forbade fine as he had all the premises for life. The same was granted in open court and Thomas was then admitted. Fine 23d by the pledge of Gilbert Russheton.

Forest of Rossyndale

Inquisition taken there for the Queen to make enquiry upon the oaths of John Ormerod, junior, George Hargreaves, Oliver Ormerod, Dionysius Hauworth of Constableleigh, Richard Crawshaie of Dedwenclough, John Wullfinden, Henry

7

Kirshaie, John Lord als. Bolton, Lawrence Tailior, Oliver Ormerod of Crawshayboith, Edward Tailior, Ellis Cunlyff, Christopher Hargreaves, James Wallm'sley, Robert Ryley, Hugh Duckeworth and Richard Wallm'sley.

Rossindale

Lawrence Rawstorne, gent., was elected greave of Rossindale
The late wife of Robert Whitacar of Rocklyff (4d) because she often [kept? *verb omitted*] vagabonds and slayers of people with her at night.
Richard Pemberton was elected greave of Accrington New Hold.
Amercements 4d.

Accrington New Hold

George Waddington surrendered by Ellis Cunlyff, greave of Accrington, one messuage and 20½ acres of land in Frerehill in Accrington New Hold, annual rent to the Queen 4s 6d, to Ambrose Kenyon and Katherine Byrtwisill and their assigns for life. Admittance sought and granted. Fine 9s by the pledge of Ellis Cunlyff.

Rossindale

Certain messuages, other buildings, lands and tenements in Dedwenclough, Wullfinden and Henherds in the Forest of Rossindale, annual rent to the Queen 2s 2½d ¼d, came into the Queen's hands by the death of Richard Tailior. Richard Tailior was his son and next heir and of full age. Admittance sought and granted. Fine 2s 2½d ¼d by the pledge of Richard Crawshaye.

Afterwards, the said Richard Tailior surrendered the property to the use of Lawrence, son of John Nuttall of Newalheigh, and his heirs for ever. Admittance sought and granted. Fine 2s 2½d ¼d by the pledge of Richard Crawshaye.

George Nuttall and Francis Nuttall surrendered by Richard Smythez, deputy steward for John Towneley, esq., one messuage, other buildings and one parcel of land, meadow, grazing land, pasture, moor and moss in le Okenheadwood in the Forest of Rossindale, annual rent to the Queen 21s 8d, and now or lately in the tenure of the said George Nuttall and Joan Hauworth, widow, to Thomas Holden and his heirs for ever. Admittance sought and granted. Fine 21s 8d by the pledge of Lawrence Nuttall.

Afterwards, the said Thomas Hollden surrendered the property to the use of Francis, son of John Nuttall of Newalheigh, his heirs and assigns, for ever. Admittance sought and granted. Fine 21s 8d by the pledge of Lawrence Nutter [*sic*], brother of the said Francis.

Dionysius Hauworth, greave of Rossindale, surrendered one messuage, other buildings, lands, tenements, meadows, grazing lands, pastures, moors and mosses in Wullfindenboth, Wulfinden and Henhards in the Forest of Rossindale, annual rent to the Queen 7s 8½d which is piecemeal[?], which Edmund Assheworth of Wullfindenboth delivered to him, to Oliver Assheworth, son of the said Edmund, and his heirs and assigns for ever. Admittance sought. The said Edmund forbade fine as he had all the premises for life and because Alice, his wife, had her reasonable dower from the premises after Edmund's death. The same was granted in open court and Oliver was then admitted. Fine 7s 8½d which is piecemeal [?] by the pledge of Owen Assheworth.

Edmund Assheworth of Wullfindenboith surrendered by Dionysius Hauworth, greave of Rossindale, one mansion house, now or lately in the occupation of the said Edmund, in [blank] in the Forest of Rossindale, annual rent to the Queen 2d, to William, James, Robert and John Assheworth, sons of the said Edmund, for life. Admittance sought and granted. Fine 2d by the pledge of John Tailior.

Francis Nuttall surrendered certain messuages, other buildings, lands, tenements, meadows, grazing lands, and pastures in Dedwenclough, Wullfinden and Henhead in the Forest of Rossindale, annual rent to the Queen 8s 10½d ¼d, to Lawrence Nuttall, brother of the said Francis, his heirs and assigns for ever. Admittance sought and granted. Fine 8s 10½d ¼d by the pledge of Gilbert Russheton.

[Membrane 3]

John Ormerod of Gamblesyde, junior, surrendered by George Hargreaves, greave of Rossindale, one messuage, other buildings, lands, tenements, meadows, grazing lands, pastures, moors and mosses in Gamblesyde and Wullfynden in the Forest of Rossindale, annual rent to the Queen 42s 1½d and the third part of ½d, to Peter Ormerod, son of the said John, as feofee according to an indenture dated [blank] and made by (1) the said John and (2) Peter Ormerod. Admittance sought. Henry Ormerod, brother of the said Peter, and Isabel, his wife, forbade fine as they had a certain parcel of the premises previously granted to them. The said Peter found pledge George Ormerod to answer the forbid and admittance was then granted. Fine 42s 1½d and the third part of ½d by the pledge aforesaid.

Haslingden

Ellen, daughter of Richard Roithwell of Haslingden, surrendered by Adam Hollden, deputy greave of Haslingden, and Robert Dureden, tenant of the Queen, half of one close or parcel of land called Heigh holme in Haslingden containing half of one rood of land, and now in the tenure of Adam Roithwell, to Elizabeth Roithwell, wife of the said Adam, and sister of the said Ellen, and her heirs for ever. Admittance sought and granted. Fine ½d by the pledge of John Nuttowe.

Francis Garside, gent., and Robert Dureden, tenants of the Queen, surrendered one messuage, other buildings and 11 acres of land in Haslingden in a certain place there called Brodeholden which George Nevell, esq., delivered to them, to Henry Hargreaves and his heirs for ever. Admittance sought and granted. Fine 3s by the pledge of Francis Garsyd.

Francis Garsyd, gent., and Robert Dureden, tenants of the Queen, surrendered half of one messuage and 2 acres of land with other buildings in Haslingden. And also another parcel of land in Ugden, annual rent to the Queen 8d, which George Nevell delivered to them, to William Roithwell and his heirs for ever. Admittance sought and granted. Fine 8d, fine in Ugden 8d by the pledge of Robert Dureden.

Francis Garsid, gent., and Robert Dureden, tenants of the Queen, surrendered half of one messuage and other buildings and 2 acres of land in Haslingden. And also a parcel of land in Ugden, annual rent to the Queen 8d, which George Nevell, esq., delivered to them, to John Roithwell, son of Ellis Roithwell, and his heirs for ever. Admittance sought. Gilbert Roithwell forbade fine as he had all of the property for life. The same was granted to him in open court by the said John Roithwell who was then admitted. Fine 8d, fine in Ugden 8d by the pledge of John Nuttowe.

Francis Garsyd, gent., and Robert Dureden, tenants of the Queen, surrendered one messuage, other buildings and 11 acres of land in Haslingden, which George Nevell of Ragnell, esq., delivered to them, to Henry Heape and John, his son, for ever as feofees according to the intent. Admittance sought and granted. Fine 3s 8d by the pledge of Francis Garsyd, gent.

The intent was that the feofees were to be seised of half of the property to the use of [blank], wife of the said Henry Heape, for life, and of the other half to the use of [blank], wife of the said John Heape, (if she happened to survive the said Henry and John, her husband), for life. The remainder of the whole of the premises to the use of the said Henry and John Heape for their lives and after their deaths then to the right heirs of the said John for ever.

Rossindale

Alice Lawe, relict of Edmund Lawe, by Oliver Lawe, her attorney, complained against Ralph Hauworth of Musburye in a plea of dower, viz that the defendant withheld the plaintiff's dower, that is to say the fourth part of one messuage and other buildings, and 60 acres of land, meadow, grazing land and pasture in the park of Musbury[1] in the Forest of Rossindale, annual rent to the Queen 32s 6d, now or lately in the tenure of the said Ralph Hauworth. The defendant denied this. The jury of John Robinson, John Cronckeshey, John Hartley of Bareley, John Mankenholes, John Robinson of Roughleigh, Nicholas Robinson, junior, John Smyth, Nicholas Bawdwen, Robert Hartley, Roger Harteley, Henry Harteley, Lawrence Robt., Gilbert Byrtwisill, Thurstan Byrtwisill, John Assheworth, Oliver Ormerod of Wullfinden, Oliver Romesbothom of Okenheadwood, Edward Tailior, William Yate of Hoddlesden, junior, James Hollden, Edward Ryley, Hugh Duckworth, Robert Ryley and Oliver Ormerod of Crawshayboith found that the defendant had withheld the plaintiff's dower. Thus the plaintiff was to take possession and the defendant was in mercy. Amercement 3d.

Sum of this halmote £8 9s 7d and half of ¼d approved.

---

[1] Musbury was enclosed as a deer park in 1304-5. In 1507 it was divided up into eight parcels of 60 customary acres each and developed as farmland.

Accrington
**Halmote of the manor of Accryngton held there Friday, 17th June, 11
Elizabeth I [1569] before John Towneley, esq., chief steward there.**

Inquisition taken there of the Old Hold for the Queen to make enquiry upon the
oaths of Ralph Hollden, esq., Francis Garsyd, gent., Robert Dureden, Richard
Dureden, Robert Heigh, Charles Gregory, Richard Rothewell, junior, John Heap,
junior, Ralph Russheton, John Kenyon, Thomas Ryley, John Byrtwisill, Giles
Whitacar, Richard Aitehaulgh, and Robert Ryley, senior.

Accrington Old Hold
   The fourth part of one house and the fourth part of one rood of land in
Accrington Old Hold came into the Queen's hands by the death of Katherine
Jackeson. Christopher Jackeson was her kinsman [*'consanguinus'*] and next heir
and of full age. Admittance sought and granted. Fine ¼d by the pledge of John
Whitacarr.

Haslingden
   George Hargreaves surrendered by Adam Hollden, greave of Haslingden, the
fourth part of one rood of land in Brodehollden in Haslingden, to Richard
Hargreaves, junior, and his heirs for ever. Admittance sought and granted. Fine ¼d
by the pledge of the said Adam Hollden.

                              [Membrane 3d]

Rossindale
   Robert Asheworth, Jane, his wife and Arthur Assheworth surrendered by
Dionysius Hauworth, greave of Rossindale, half of one messuage, other buildings,
and half of one parcel of land, meadow, grazing land, pasture and moss in Cowopp
in the Forest of Rossindale called Cowopp Craighead, annual rent to the Queen 12d,
now or lately in the tenure of Gilbert Hill, to Francis, son of John Nuttall of
Newhalhey and his assigns from the feast of St. Michael the Archangel [29th
September] next for twenty-four years. Admittance sought and granted. Fine 12d by
the pledge of John Nuttall.
   Christopher Bridge of Bacopp surrendered by Dionysius Hauworth, greave of
Rossindale, certain messuages, lands, tenements, meadows, grazing lands, pastures
and mosses in Bacoppboth, Horelawehead and Wullfinden in the Forest of
Rossindale, annual rent to the Queen 6s 4½d and two parts of ¼d, to the use of
Edmund Robtshawe, illegitimate son of Thomas Rob'tshaw, as feofee according to
the intent. Admittance sought and granted. Fine 6s 4½d and two parts of ¼d by the
pledge of John Lord als. Bollton.
   The intent was that Edmund Rob'tshawe and his heirs were to be seised of the
property to the use of Alice Rob'tshaie, wife of the above-named Thomas Robtshay
and mother to the said Edmund, for life. And after her death to the use of the said
Edmund Rob'tshaie and his heirs for ever.

Christopher Bridge of Bacopp surrendered by Dionysius Hauworth, greave of Rossindale, certain messuages, buildings, lands and tenements in Bacoppbothe, Horelawehead and Wullfinden in the Forest of Rossindale, annual rent to the Queen 2½d and two parts of ¼d, to Isabel Robtshawe, widow, and her heirs, for ever. Admittance sought and granted. Fine 2½d and two parts of ¼d by the pledge of John Wallton.

Christopher Bridge of Bacopp surrendered by Dionysius Hauworth, greave of Rossindale, certain messuages, other buildings, lands, tenements, meadows, grazing lands and pastures in Bacoppboth, Howlawhead and Wullfinden in the Forest of Rossindale, annual rent to the Queen 15¼d and the third part of ¼d, to Jennet, now wife of John Lord als. Bollton, and her heirs for ever. Admittance sought and granted. Fine 15¼d and the third part of ¼d by the pledge of John Lord als. Bollton.

Forest of Rossindale
Inquisition taken there of the Forest for the Queen to make enquiry upon the oaths of John Ormerod, junior, George Dureden, Oliver Pilling, Oliver Ormerod of Crawshayboth, James Hauworth, Dionysius Hauworth of Constableligh, Christopher Bridge of Dedwenclough, George Nuttall, Owen Assheworth, John Tattersall, junior, Christopher Bridge of Bacopp, Lawrence Tailior, Oliver Romesbothome of Okenheadwood, Christopher Hargreaves, James Gryme, Richard Wallmsley, Robert Hauworth and Henry Hollden.

Oliver Ormerod, Oliver Romesbothome, Owen Assheworth and Robert Lord were elected fence lookers in Rossindale; Richard Assheworth and Thomas Whitworth were elected pounders; George Ryley and Hugh Duckworth were elected fence lookers in Accrington.

Rossindale
Miles Heap (20d) because he made an affray upon Thomas Rawstorne.

John Sedden (12d) and Dorothy Sedden (12d) because they broke the Queen's fold at Dedwenclough.

Amercements 3s 8d.

Rossindale
At the halmote of the manor of Accrington held there on Thursday, 17th June, 4 Elizabeth I [1562] before the steward aforesaid, John Lawe of Tunsted surrendered by John Nuttowe and John Lorde als. Jenken, tenants of the Queen, two houses and certain lands, tenements, meadows, grazing lands, pastures and mosses in Tunsted, Sedge and Soweclough in the Forest of Rossindale, annual rent to the Queen 7s 4d, now or lately in the tenure of the said John Lawe. That is to say one house in a certain meadow on the east side of the main barn of the said John Lawe and one other house in le Soweclough and half of all arable land, meadows, grazing lands,

pastures and mosses in le Tunsted, Sedge and Soweclough of which John Lawe was seised according to the custom of the manor, to Lawrence Hollden of Accrington, Nicholas, his son, John Tattersall, of Tunsted, junior, and John Lorde, son of James Lord als. Bolton, and their heirs, for ever as feofees according to the intent. Admittance sought and granted. Fine 14s 8d by the pledge of John Lord Bolton [*sic*].

The intent was that the feofees were to be seised of the property to the use of the said John Lawe and Isabel, his wife, for their lives. If John and Isabel died within sixteen years of the date hereof, then the feofees were to take all issues, profits, rents and revenues from the property for the remainder of the sixteen years towards the redemption 'lowsing or acquiting owt' of certain lands, tenements, meadows, mosses and pastures in Wullfinden in the occupation of the late wife of George Lawe, from Hugh Hallsted and his heirs. And the same so redeemed were to be to the use of John Lawe of Wullfinden, son of George Lawe, deceased, and his heirs for ever. The remainder of the said two houses, etc. after the deaths of the said John and Isabel Lawe of Tunsted and the end of the sixteen years, was to be to the use of John Lawe of Wullfinden and his lawfully begotten heirs. And in default of such issue then to the use of 'Ranallde' Lawe, one of the other sons of the said George Lawe, and his heirs for ever. And also if the said John Lawe of Wullfinden when he reached the age of twenty-four or within six months following (if he happened to live so long) came into the court of the manor of Accrington and before the steward confessed that neither he nor any other person in his name nor by his consent nor procurement would vex nor trouble Thomas Lawe nor Gilbert Lawe, his uncles, concerning any lands or hereditaments which the said John Lawe, their father, gave to them jointly or severally, or if the said John Lawe of Wullfinden happened to die without lawful issue before he reached the age of twenty-four, that then if the said 'Raynold' Lawe, when he reached the age of twenty-four or within six months following, came into the court of the manor of Accrington and made the same confession, then the estates limited to the said John and 'Ranold', sons of the said George, were to stand and be in full power. Provided always that if John and 'Raynold' Lawe did not come before the steward as aforesaid, then from thenceforth the feofees were to be seised of the premises after the deaths of John and Isabel Lawe and the end of the sixteen years to the use of the said Thomas Lawe and Gilbert Lawe, their heirs and assigns for ever.

Accrington New Hold

Ambrose Rusheton complained against Ralph Wallm'sley and George Wallm'sley, heirs of Thomas Wallm'sley, in a plea of trespass because they illegally and contrary to the custom of the manor used and frequented a way through the plaintiff's land and tenement called le Cowehouseheigh and furthermore the defendants had used the way for many years. The defendants denied this. The jury of twenty-four customary tenants of the New Hold, that is to say, Richard Woodrof,

Christopher Harteley, John Mitton, Edmund Stevenson, John Cronckeshey, Edward Hargreaves, Lawrence Shuttleworth, Lawrence Robt., James Hartley, Geoffrey Hartley, James Harteley, Roger Harteley, Oliver Ormerod of Crawshaieboth, John Pillinge of Brockeclough, William Jenkinson, Hugh Pillinge of Tunsted, James Whitacar of Bacopp, Thomas Duckworth, James Piccopp, John Hauworth, Christopher Hargreaves, Edward Ryley, junior, Robert Ryley and Edmund Pillinge found that the defendants did not use the way illegally and contrary to the custom of the manor. Thus the plaintiff was in mercy for a false plea. Amercement 1d.

Rossindale

At the halmote of the manor of Accrington held there on 17th June 8 Elizabeth I [1566] before the steward, William Kenyon, gent., surrendered one messuage and other buildings, lands and tenements in Dedwenclough, Wullfinden and Henheads in the Forest of Rossindale, annual rent to the Queen 8s 8½d, to Francis Nuttall and his heirs for ever. Admittance sought and granted. Fine 8s 8½d by the pledge of Barnard Towneley.

[Membrane 4]

George Dureden, greave of Rossindale, surrendered the third part of one messuage, other buildings, lands, tenements, meadows, grazing lands, pastures and mosses in Loveclough, Henhead and Frerehill in the Forest of Rossindale, annual rent to the Queen 17s ½d, which Richard Byrtwisill of Loveclough delivered to him, to George Hargreaves, Francis Dureden and Oliver Ormerod of Gamblesyd as feofees according to the intent. Admittance sought. Gilbert Byrtwisill forbade fine by the right of his inheritance. George Hargreaves and his co-feofees found pledges John Nuttall and Hugh Hallstead to answer the forbid and admittance was then granted. Fine 17s ½d by the pledges aforesaid.

The intent was that the feofees were to be seised of the property to the use of the said Richard Birtwisill for life and after his death to the use of Jennet, his wife, if she survived him, during the minority and 'nonage' of William Byrtwisill, son of the said Richard, for the better education and bringing up of the children lawfully begotten of the said Richard, if the said Jennet kept herself sole and unmarried. After the said William Byrtwisill reached the age of twenty-one, the feofees were to be seised of half of the premises to the use of the said William, his heirs and assigns for ever, and of the other half to the use of the said Jennet for life if she kept herself sole and unmarried. The remainder of the second half to the use of the said William, his heirs and assigns for ever.

Francis Gerside, gent., surrendered certain messuages, other buildings, lands and tenements, meadows, grazing lands, pastures, and mosses in Crawshayboth, Lawnde of Crydden, backside of Crydden and Henheades in the Forest of Rossindale, annual rent to the Queen 15s 1½d. That is to say the seventh part of all messuages, other buildings, lands, etc. lying on the south side of Crawshaiboith and on the east side of the great stream of water flowing down by the vaccary[1] of

---

[1]   A vaccary was originally a cattle farm established by the Earl of Lincoln in the 13th century.

Crawshaieboth called Crawshaiboth Water, now or lately in the tenure of Lettice Ormerod, widow, and Oliver Ormerod. And the third part of all messuages, other buildings, lands, etc. in Lawnd of Crydden and Backeside of Crydden now or lately in the tenure of Henry Hauworth, Richard Mankenhoiles, George Gregory, Richard Gregory, Miles Hole and the said Lettice Ormerod and Oliver Ormerod. And one parcel of the pasture of Henheades of the annual rent of 1½d, to Hugh Hallstead, gent., his heirs and assigns for ever. Admittance sought and granted. Fine 15s 1½d by the pledge of John Nuttowe.

Robert Asheworth of Cowopp and Jane, his wife, surrendered by Dionysius Hauworth, greave of Rossindale, half of one messuage, other buildings and half of a parcel of land, meadow, grazing land, pasture and moss in Cowopp called le Cradgehead in the Forest of Rossindale, annual rent to the Queen 12d, now or lately in the tenure of Gilbert Hill, to Francis Nuttall, his heirs and assigns for ever. Admittance sought and granted. Fine 12d by the pledge of John Nuttall.

Francis Hollte, esq., complained against John Lawe, Gilbert Lawe, John Tattersall of Tunsted, junior, John Lorde als. Jenken and John Lorde als. Bollton in a plea of partition of one close of land called le Ov'heigh in Tunsted in the Forest of Rossindale, in the tenure of Richard Nuttowe, the said John Lawe and Gilbert Lawe. The jury of Robert Assheworth of Fearnes, John Wullfinden, James Tattersall, Henry Kyrshey, Edmund Lache, George Dureden, Gilbert Byrtwisill, Dionysius Hauworthe, Oliver Romesbothome, Edward Tailior, Owen Schofeild and Edmund Assheworth als. Chicken found that the said Francis Holt had and ought to have the west part of the said close of land called Overheigh and the aforesaid John Lawe and Gilbert Lawe had and ought to have the west [sic] part of the said close of land. Therefore the defendants were in mercy. Amercement 2d.

Gilbert Lawe, son of John Lawe of Tunsted, complained against Francis Hollt, esq., Christopher Nuttowe, Dionysius Hauworth, Francis Garsyd, junior, John Cowopp and Richard Nuttowe in a plea of trespass because the defendants illegally and contrary to the custom of the manor occupied certain ways through the plaintiff's land and tenement from which it deteriorated and suffered damage to the value of 40s. The defendants denied this. The jury of the said Robert Assheworth and the other jurors aforesaid found that the defendants used the ways rightly and justly and not illegally or unjustly. Therefore the plaintiff was in mercy for a false plea. Amercement 1d.

Margaret Hasilham, widow, complained against Henry Cunluf of Dedwenclough in a plea of land because the said Henry unjustly, illegally and contrary to the custom of the manor detained from the plaintiff for a long time the sixth part of one messuage, other buildings, lands and tenements in Dedwenclough in the Forest of Rossindale, annual rent to the Queen 30s and the third part of ½d. The defendant denied this. The jury of James Hauworth, Oliver Ormerod of Crawshaieboth, George Hargreaves of Wullfinden, James Piccopp, John Lorde als. Bollton, John Pillinge of Tunsted, Edmund Romesbothome, Oliver Romesbothome,

Henry Hollden, Hugh Duckworth, Robert Ryley and Edward Ryley, junior, found that the defendant had detained the property and was therefore in mercy. Amercement 1d.

Christopher Bridge of Greaveclough, Christopher Bridge of Dedwenclough and Thomas Lawe, survivors of George Lawe, at the request of Edmund Tailior of Wullfindenbothe, surrendered by Lawrence Rawstorne, gent., tenant of the Queen, one messuage, other buildings, lands and tenements, meadows, grazing lands, pastures and mosses in Wullfindenboth, annual rent to the Queen 8s 11d and 1½d of rent in Henheades, in the Forest of Rossindale, to John Tailior, son of the said Edmund, his heirs and assigns, for ever. Admittance sought. The said Edmund forbade fine as he had two parts of the premises for life. This was granted to him in open court by the said John who was then admitted. Fine 9s ½d by the pledge of George Ormerod.

The same people surrendered one messuage, other buildings, lands, tenements, meadows, grazing lands, pastures and mosses in Wullfinden in the Forest of Rossindale, annual rent to the Queen 6s 4d, and one parcel of the pasture of Henheades, annual rent 1½d, to James Tailior, younger son of the said Edmund, his heirs and assigns, for ever. Admittance sought. The said Edmund forbade fine as he had all of the premises for life. This was granted to him in open court by the said James who was then admitted. Fine 6s 4d [*sic*] by the pledge of Gilbert Lawe.

At the halmote of the manor of Accrington held there on Thursday, 8th June, 4 Elizabeth I [1562] before the steward aforesaid, Charles Nuttowe surrendered by James Whitacar, then greave of Rossindale, one messuage, other buildings, lands, tenements, meadows, grazing lands, pastures and mosses in Cowopp in the Forest of Rossindale, annual rent to the Queen 21s 3d, now or lately in the tenure of James Assheworth, to the said James Assheworth and his heirs for ever. Admittance sought and granted. Fine 21s 3d by the pledge of John Nuttall.

[*Membrane 4d*]

At the halmote of the manor of Accrington held there on Thursday, 12th December, 9 Elizabeth I [1566] before the steward aforesaid it was presented by inquisition that one messuage, other buildings and certain lands, tenements, meadows, grazing lands, pastures and mosses in Crawshaybothe and Henheades in the Forest of Rossindale, annual rent to the Queen 25s 3d, came into the Queen's hands by the death of John Hauworth of Crawshayboith. George Hauworth was his son and next heir and aged about nineteen years and Dionysius Hauworth was his guardian. Admittance was sought. Agnes, lately wife of the said John Hauworth, forbade fine as she had a reasonable dower in the premises according to the custom of the manor. George found pledge, the said Dionysius, to answer the forbid and admittance was then granted. Fine 25s 3d by the pledge aforesaid.

At the halmote of the manor of Accrington held there on Thursday, 12th December, 9 Elizabeth I [1566] before the steward aforesaid it was presented by inquisition that John Hauworth, late of Crawshayboth, died about the date of the last court seised in reversion of one messuage, other buildings, lands, tenements, meadows, grazing lands, pastures and mosses in Crawshayboith and Henhead, on the south side of Crawshayboith in the Forest of Rossindale, annual rent to the Queen 6s 8d. George Hauworth was his son and next heir and aged about nineteen years and Dionysius Hauworth, junior, was his guardian. Admittance was sought. Agnes, lately wife of the said John Hauworth, forbade fine as she had a reasonable dower in the premises. George found pledge, the said Dionysius, to answer the forbid and admittance was then granted. Fine 6s 8d by the pledge aforesaid.

Sum of this halmote £6 18s 1d approved

Sum total of the two said halmotes £15 7s 8d
Approved and charged in the 11th year of Queen Elizabeth
Haselingden 15s 8½d; fines for land 10s 4½d, amercements 5s 4d
Acrington Old Hold 36s 7¼d total of fines
Acrington New Hold 9s 1d viz fines for land 9s, amercements 1d
Rossendale £12 6s 3d; fines for land £12 20d, amercements 4s 7d

Colne
Halmote of the manor of Colne held there Thursday, 9th December, 11 Elizabeth I [1568] before John Towneley, esq., chief steward there.

Inquisition taken there for the Queen to make enquiry upon the oaths of Thomas Emot, John Blakey, John Hargreaves, senior, Christopher Dicconson, John Folldes, James Smyth, John Ellot, John Robinson of Goldshay, John Tailior, William Harteley, John Mankenhoyles, Gilbert Hartley, Edmund Rydehaulgh, James Willson, Henry Harteley and Lawrence Willson.

Thomas Emot was elected greave of Colne; Lawrence Ingh'm was elected constable of Colne; Miles Parker was elected constable of the vill of Colne and Richard Bollton was elected constable of M'sden.

John Forster (6d) because he turned a watercourse from its right course into a contrary one to the damage of his neighbours.
Amercements 6d.

John Whitacar, gent., and Thomas Robinson, feofees, Alice Radclif, widow, and Thomas Radclif, esq., now deceased, at the request of Gilbert Gerrard, esq., the Queen's attorney general, and Anne, his wife and daughter of the said Thomas Radclif deceased, surrendered by William Hanson, greave of Colne, one messuage called Greswall and also certain messuages and tenements called le Brigeholme, lez Hulhill, lez Wormeleewes near to Wallferden on the south side of Catlowe containing 17 acres of rodeland and 1 acre of new improvement lying near one close. And also one piece of land containing 6 acres and 4½ acres of land called Catlawe grene lying on the east side of Catlawe in Great M'sden. And also 30 acres of land, one toft, 5½ acres 1 rood of land in Great Marsden within the halmote of Colne, to the said Gilbert Gerrard and Anne, his wife, and the heirs of the said Anne. Admittance sought by Gilbert and Anne through their attorney, John Braddill, esq., and it was granted. Fine 21s 5d by the pledges of Nicholas Mitchell and Robert Robinson.

Alexander Russheworth, gent., surrendered by John Foldes, tenant of the Queen, three messuages, three gardens and 1½ acres of land in Colne. And also 1½ acres of land in le Vyver in Colne. And also one other acre of land in Great M'sden, to James Folldes of Trawden and his heirs for ever. Admittance sought. Nicholas Walker forbade fine by right of his inheritance. John Walker forbade fine by right of his inheritance. James Folldes found pledge Edward M'sden to answer the forbids and admittance was then granted. Fine 16d by the pledge aforesaid.

Inquisition taken there of the Forest for the Queen to make enquiry upon the oaths of Lawrence Shutleworth of Wynewall, Lawrence Rob't of the same, John Dryver of the same, Roger Harteley of Wycolar, Bernard Hartley of the same, Christopher Harteley of the same, James Emote of the same, Robert Harteley of Trawden, Richard Harteley of the same, Geoffrey Hartley of the same, Geoffrey Shacleden of the same, junior, Richard Shacleden of the same, Lawrence Hartley of the same and James Hartley of the same, junior.

Richard Harteley was elected greave of Trawden.

Henry Mytton (2d), Geoffrey Shawe (2d), James Prymet (2d), Geoffrey Rycrofte (2d), William Boitheman (2d) and James Foldes of Ley (2d) because they tore out and uprooted gorse and heath upon Bulsmore.

Edmund Hartley (2d) because he overstocked le Oxclose in Trawden.
Amercements 14d

Geoffrey Shacleden of Trawden, junior, surrendered by James Harteley, greave of Trawden, one messuage, other buildings, lands, tenements, meadows, grazing lands, and pastures with moors and mosses in the Forest of Trawden, annual rent to the Queen 20s 10d, now or lately in the tenure of the said Geoffrey Shacleden, to James Shacleden, son and heir apparent of the said Geoffrey. Admittance sought. The said Geoffrey forbade fine for himself and Margaret, his wife, because he had two parts of the premises for life and she had her dower in the premises according to the custom of the manor. The same was granted to them by James in open court and he was then admitted. Fine 20s 10d by the pledge of James Foldes.

[Membrane 5]

Christopher Hargreaves, citizen and grocer of London, complained by his attornies, Ralph Russheton, esq., and Hugh Hallsted, gent., against Robert Robinson of Oldlaund in a plea of land, viz the defendant detained from the plaintiff unjustly, illegally and without right one messuage and other buildings and 9 acres 3 roods of land in Great M'sden in the tenure of John Clayton. The defendant denied this. The jury of Francis Garsyd, gent., Robert Dureden, Robert Gregory, Thomas Ryley, John Kenyon, Christopher Jackeson, John Houghton, Thomas Whitwham, Giles Whitacar, Christopher Smyth, Hugh Tailior, Miles Aspeden, Richard Kendall, junior, John Dawson of Chatburne, John Spenser, John Wullton, John Dawson of Wurstone, Christopher Migecock, James Smyth of Edg, John Hartley, Edward Marsden, Christopher Dicconson, John Hartley of Adm'gill and John Harryson found that the defendant did not detain the premises from the plaintiff. Therefore the plaintiff was in mercy. Amercement 3d.

[*The above entry is followed by the enrolment of Christopher Hargreaves's letter of attorney dated 10th December 9 Elizabeth I [1566] by which he appointed Ralph Russheton of Dunkenhaulgh, esq., and Hugh Hallstead of Habergh'meves, gent., his attornies.*]

Sum of this halmote 45s 6d approved.

Colne
Halmote of the manor of Colne held there Tuesday, 26th April, 11 Elizabeth I [1569] before John Towneley, esq., chief steward there.

Inquisition taken there of the Old Hold for the Queen to make enquiry upon the oaths of Henry Banester, gent., Thomas Emot, Edward M'sden, Henry Shawe, James Smyth, John Wallton, William Hanson, John Dryver, John Tailior, John Mankenholes, Lawrence Willson, Henry Wallton, Henry Hartley, Robert Bawdwen and James Willson.

The jurors said that they had found nothing to present because all was well.

John Hartley of Swinden surrendered, by Robert Hartley of Great M'sden, a tenant of the Queen, one messuage, other buildings, and 20½ acres of arable land and meadow, being a parcel of the demesne land of Swynden aforesaid in Great Mersden, in the tenure of the said John Hartley, and his assigns, to John Talior of Cloughhead, Roger Hartley, son and heir apparent of James Hartley of Wynewall and their heirs as feofees according to the intent. Admittance sought and granted. Fine 6s 10d by the pledge of John Swayne.

The intent was that the feofees were to be seised of the property to the use of the said John Hartley for life and after his death to the uses given in his last will and testament.

John Swane surrendered one messuage and one close of land called Bent Heigh containing 2 acres of land in Great M'sden, in the tenure of the said John Swaine, to Lawrence Leche and his assigns for life. Admittance sought and granted. An annual rent of 2d was payable to John Swane and his heirs. Fine 8d by the pledge of John Tailior.

John Mitchell surrendered one messuage and one garden in Colne, annual rent to the Queen 3d, to Nicholas Mitchell of Walkefeild and his heirs for ever. Admittance sought. John Scale forbade fine by right of his inheritance. Nicholas Mitchell found pledge Nicholas Mitchell of Olde Earth to answer the forbid and was then admitted. Fine 3d by the pledge aforesaid.

James Foldes (at the request of Elizabeth Emot, widow, Thomas, son of Nicholas Emote, and William Emot), surrendered one messuage and other buildings and 10 acres of land in Emot lone within the jurisdiction of the said halmote, late in the tenure of the said Elizabeth, to the said Thomas Emot and his lawfully begotten heirs and in default of such issue, remainder thereof to the said William Emot and his heirs for ever. Admittance sought by the said Thomas and William. Elizabeth forbade fine as she had the premises for life. This was granted to her in open court by the said Thomas and William who were then admitted. Fine 3s 4d by the pledge of James Folldes.

Thomas Emott of Emott Lone complained against Elizabeth Emott, widow, Thomas Emott and James Foldes in a plea of land, viz of one messuage, other buildings and 9 acres of land in Emot Lone within the jurisdiction of this manor, being the plaintiff's inheritance. The defendants denied this. The jury of twenty-four customary tenants of the Old Hold consisting of John Higgen of M'sden, John Whitacar of Mickilhurste, Robert Whitacar of Healey, James Bancrofte, Charles Wood, John Hargreaves, Robert Dureden, Richard Roithewell, John Bentley, Robert Ryley, John Ryding, John Ormerod, Richard Kendall, senior, Richard Kendall, junior, John Hyrde, John Harryson, William Hodson, John More, Henry Wallton, junior, Christopher Dicconson, Nicholas Mitchell of Old Earth, Nicholas Mytchell of Colne, William Hartley of Bradley and John Ellot of Edge found that the defendants did not disseise the plaintiff of the premises. Thus the plaintiff was in mercy for a false plea. Amercement 3d.

[*Membrane 5d*]

Thomas Russheworth, gent., surrendered by Robert Hirste, greave of Colne, and John Foldes, a tenant of the Queen, one capital messuage called le Stanrodhall, 21 acres of rodeland, 1½ roods of land called Stanrod with le lones lying in Colne. And also 52 acres of land called le Carrheys in the Forest of Trawden of the Old Hold, in the tenure of John Russheworth, father of the said Thomas, esq., and his assigns, to Edward M'sden, James Folldes of Trawden, Nicholas Mitchell of Colne, son of Richard, and John Blakey of Colne, junior, and their heirs for ever as feofees according to the intent. Admittance sought and granted. Fine 48s 11d by the pledge of Robert Robinson.

The intent was that the feofees were to be seised of the capital messuage called Stanrodehall and the rest of the premises to the use of the said John Russheworth, esq., and his assigns for life. After his death they were to be seised to the use of the said Thomas Russheworth and his lawful heirs. In default of such issue, they were to be seised to the use of John Russheworth, younger, and his lawful heirs. In default of such issue, they were to be seised to the use of Robert Russheworth and his lawful heirs with remainder in default of such issue to the right heirs of the said John Russheworth, the elder, for ever.

Nicholas Mitchell of Colne, a tenant of the Queen, surrendered one messuage, other buildings and two closes of land called Blackestubeies and one messuage and other buildings in le Holme and le Hagg called Brownhilbancke, one other close of land called Lower Walkrfeld and one other close called Nether Heigh, in the tenure of John Blakey, senior, lying on the north side of Pullforth. And also 6 acres of land in Alkencotes within the vill of Coln. All of which premises were within the jurisdiction of this halmote and contained 38 acres and were delivered to him by Henry Forror, son of Henry Farror of Ewood, Richard Nayler, son of Thomas Nailer and John Horsfall of Stoidley, at the request of Margaret Blakey, widow. To Ellen, now wife of Henry Farror, gent., and daughter of Robert Blakey, late deceased, and her heirs for ever. Admittance sought. The said Margaret Blakey, widow, by James Bawdewen, forbade fine for her dower for life and it was granted to her by the said Ellen in open court. John Blakey of Colne, senior, forbade fine by right of his inheritance and Ellen found pledges John Swane and William Hanson to answer the forbid. Admittance was then granted. Fine 12s 8d by the pledges aforesaid.

Afterwards, the said Ellen Faror, now wife of Henry Farror, gent., surrendered the premises to the use of Ambrose, son of William Grenewood, William, son of John Grenewood, John Farror, son of Henry Ferror of Hollynheigh, and John Swayne of Southefeld, their heirs and assigns as feofees according to the intent. Admittance sought. Margaret Blakey, widow, by James Bawdwen, forbade fine for her dower for life and it was granted to her in open court. John Blakey of Colne forbade fine by right of his inheritance and Ambrose Grenewood and his co-feofees found pledge John Tailior to answer the forbid. Admittance was then granted. Fine 12s 8d by the pledge aforesaid.

The intent was that the feofees were to be seised of the property to the use of the said Henry Farror and Ellen, his wife, for their lives and after their deaths to the use of their lawful heirs. In default of such issue, then to the uses given in the last will and testament of either the said Henry or Ellen, whoever lived longest.

[*In the margin*] Amercements 3d

Sum of this halmote £4 5s 10d approved.

Sum total of the said two halmotes £6 11s 4d
Colne 109s 4d; fines for land 108s 7d, amercements 9d
Troden 22s; fines for land 20s 10d, amercements 14d
Approved and charged in the 11th year of Queen Elizabeth.

Bruneley
Halmote of the manor of Ightenhill held at Bruneley, Wednesday, 10th December, 11 Elizabeth I [1568] before John Towneley, esq., chief steward there.

Inquisition taken there for the Queen to make enquiry upon the oaths of Nicholas Harg', John Whitacar, William Folldes, Robert Roo, John Robinson of Goldshaie, John Hargreaves, John Higgyn, Henry Willysill, Richard Tattersall, William Smyth of Hill, John Hallstead of Windlehouse, William Loynd, senior, Francis Webster and George Smyth of Hollyngreave

James Dugdale of Higham (8d) because he kept his fences open, one lane insufficiently repaired and unlawfully pursued the livestock and cattle of his neighbours between Ammot Hill and Padiham.

John Robinson of Haberghameves (4d) because he diverted a watercourse there from its right course into a contrary one.

John Heigh of Padiham (3s 4d) and Thomas Willysell of Scolebanck (3s 4d) because they made an affray together.

A penalty of 20s was imposed at the last halmote that Anne Towneley, widow, lately wife of Nicholas Towneley, esq., deceased, (20d), should lay open one usual and ancient way upon and through her land and tenement called le Roylhill before the date of this halmote which she refused to do and so far had not done. Therefore she was in mercy.

Amercements 27s 8d.

[Membrane 6]

John Whitacar, gent., and Thomas Robinson, feofees, Alice Radclif, widow, and Thomas Radclif, esq., now deceased, at the request of Gilbert Gerrard, esq., the Queen's Attorney General, and Anne, his wife, daughter and heir of the said Thomas Radcliff, deceased, surrendered by John Tattersall, greave of Ightenhill, certain messuages, lands and tenements by the name of Hamstonclif and called the Chamber in Pendill, containing 40 acres of land in Little Mersden and one fulling mill called the Chamb'r mylne and 40 acres of land called Reidley alias Reidyhallois and Hawkshole in the Chase of Pendle, a parcel of Hamstoncliff called Chambr in Pendill within its boundaries. And three messuages and one close or a certain tenement called Sabden Hey containing 160 acres in the Chase of Pendill of the Old Hold, lying within the halmote of Ightenhill, to the said Gilbert Gerrard and Anne, his wife, and the heirs of the said Anne. Admittance sought by the said Gilbert and Anne through John Braddyll, esq., their attorney, and it was granted. Fine £4 by the pledge of John Robinson of Old Laund.

James Bancrofte surrendered by John Tattersall, greave of Ighte'hill, four messuages and all his other buildings and 75 acres of land in Ightenhill and

Habergh'm, to Barnerd Towneley, gent., Thomas Barcrofte of Ightenhill Parke, Edmund, son and heir apparent of Richard Tattersall of Brereclif, and Richard, son and heir apparent of Richard Wodrof of Habergh'meves, and their heirs as feofees according to the intent. Admittance sought and granted. Fine 25s by the pledge of Hugh Shuttleworth, gent.

The intent was that the feofees were to be seised of the property to the use of the said James Bancrofte for life and after his death to the uses given in his last will and testament. Provided always that the said surrender should not in any wise be prejudicial or hurtful to the Queen, her heirs or successors concerning the usual fines after the death of any tenant.

John Webster of Padiham surrendered, remised and remitted by Thomas Willysell and John Brandwood, tenants of the Queen, all right, claim, title, interest and demand which he had or should have in a rent of two pennies from a house in Padiham called Fletcher House, to Henry Ryley, gent., and his heirs for ever. Admittance sought and granted. Fine 2d by the pledge of Hugh Shuttleworth, gent.

Richard Saiger of Wallferden surrendered by John Tailior of Clough Head, a tenant of the Queen, half of one messuage and other buildings, a garden and 5½ acres of arable land and meadow in Little Mersden, in the tenure of the said Richard Sagr and his assigns, to Jennet and Isabel Saigr, his daughters, their heirs and assigns for ever. Admittance sought and granted. Fine 22d by the pledge of Lawrence Willson.

John Woodroff of Bruneley, senior, at the request of Henry Willysell of Coldewetherhouse, surrendered by Robert Towne, a tenant of the Queen, two messuages and other buildings, lands, tenements, meadows, grazing lands and pastures in M'sden called le Coldwether House containing 28½ acres, in the tenure of the said Henry Willysell and Margaret, his mother, to John Woodroff, junior, son and heir of the said John Woodroff, senior, Henry Hartley, son and heir apparent of Richard Harteley of Wheatleyboth, John Hurstwood, junior, son and heir apparent of John Hurstewood of Hurstwood, senior, and William Ingham, son of John Ingham, junior, lately deceased, and their heirs as feofees according to indentures made by (1) the said Henry Willysell and (2) the said John Hurstwood, senior, dated 5th August 10 Elizabeth I [1568]. Admittance sought and granted. Fine 9s 6d by the pledge of James Bancrofte.

Robert, son of Thomas Whitacar of Holme, gent., John Woodroff, junior, John Whitacar of Micklehurste, Robert Ingham of Fullage and Edmund, son of Richard Tattersall of Rigge, at the request of Robert Whitacar of Healey, surrendered one messuage, other buildings and 17 acres of land, a parcel of le Yatefeild, viz 8½ acres in the tenure of William Hargreaves and 8½ acres in the tenure of Edmund Leigh, to Lettice, wife of the said Robert Whitacar of Healey, and her assigns for life. Admittance sought by her attorney, Hugh Hallsted, and it was granted. Fine 5s 8d by the pledge of Barnerd Towneley.

Nicholas Banester, Richard Grymeshaie, esq., and John Grymeshay, son of the said Richard, feofees, at the request of Henry Ryley of Grene, gent., surrendered one messuage, one toft, three gardens and one croft or parcel of land in Padiham, in the tenure of Hugh Fletcher, containing 1 acre 1 rood of land, to the use of Lawrence, son and heir apparent of Henry Towneley of Barnesyde, esq., Lawrence Habergham, son and heir apparent of Richard Habergh'm, gent. Thomas, son and heir apparent of Thomas Ryley of Hunterholme, and George, son and heir apparent of Thomas Hollrod of Russheworth[?], and their assigns for ever as feofees according to the intent. Admittance sought and granted. Fine 5d by the pledge of [*blank*].

The intent was that the feofees were to be seised of the property to the use of the said Hugh Fletcher for life and after his death to the use of Agnes, his wife, and George, his son, for their lives. After their deaths, to the use of the said Henry Ryley for life and after his death to the use of John, son and heir apparent of the said Thomas Ryley, and his lawful heirs. In default of such issue, they were to be seised to the uses given in the last will and testament of the said Henry Ryley. Provided always that if the said Hugh, Agnes or George Fletcher did not pay and do to the said Henry Ryley, his heirs or assigns, such rents, boons and services as had been paid and done for the premises, and did not maintain and 'uphold tenantable' the house standing upon the same ground, then it should be lawful for the said Henry, his heirs, executors and assigns to re-enter into the premises as if this surrender had not been made.

[*Membrane 6d*]

John Webster of Padiham surrendered by Robert Roo, a tenant of the Queen, one messuage or house, one garden and one barn and 2½ acres of land along with sufficient way to carry and re-carry to and from the barn aforesaid, in the vill of Padiham, in the tenure of Miles Londisdale, to the said Miles Londisdale and his assigns for the life of the said John Webster. Admittance sought and granted. Fine 10d by the pledge of John Houghton.

John Webster of Padiham surrendered by Hugh Shuttleworth, gent., a tenant of the Queen, one close of land called Fyrewood and one parcel of land adjoining called le Slayhead containing 4 acres of oxgang land, lying in 'le westend' of Padiham, in the tenure of Francis Webster, Lawrence Whitacar and Christopher Bawdwen, to Robert Roo and his assigns for the life of the said John Webster. Admittance sought. The said Francis Webster, Christopher Bawdwen and Lawrence Whitacar forbade fine as they had all the premises for themselves and their heirs for a certain term of years. The same was granted to them in open court by Robert Roo. Admittance was then granted. Fine 16d by the pledge of Hugh Shuttleworth.

John Webster of Padiham surrendered by John Houghton, a tenant of the Queen, 1½ acres and 15 falls of land in Padiham, in the tenure of Thomas Whitacar, to the said Thomas and his assigns for the life of the said John Webster (after the end of a term of years formerly granted to the said Thomas by the said John). Admittance sought and granted. Fine 6½d by the pledge of the said John Houghton.

John Webster surrendered by John Houghton, a tenant of the Queen, 2½ acres of land called Chappellsted and Murfallonge in Padiham, in the tenure of Thomas Londisdale of Symondstone, to the said Thomas and his assigns for the life of the said John Webster (after the end of a term of twenty-one years formerly granted to the said Thomas by the said John). Admittance sought and granted. Fine 10d by the pledge of the said John Houghton.

John Robynson of Oldelaund complained against John Hargreaves of Lomyshaye in a plea of trespass because the defendant had diverted a stream from its right course into a contrary one between his land and tenement and the plaintiff's land and tenement in Little Mersden, whereby it had destroyed the fences and laid waste the plaintiff's land from which they deteriorated and were damaged to the value of 40s. The defendant denied this. The jury of Hugh Hallstead, John Tattersall, Robert Towne, Richard Acroid, Richard Pollard, Robert Ingham of Fullage, Miles Aspeden, John Jackson, Thomas Boithe, Lawrence Willson, John Swayne and Christopher Smyth found that John Hargreaves had diverted the stream. They also said that John Robynson ought to make and maintain his fences between his land and the defendant's land in a sufficient manner. The defendant was in mercy. Amercement 1d.

Barnerd Towneley of Hurstwood, gent., John Woodrof, senior, John Robinson of Olld Lawnd, Richard Tattersall of Rige and George Smyth of Hollyn Greave, at the request of Robert Glov' of Hallton de le Hill in Craven, in the county of York, yeoman, surrendered by William Hallsted of Bankehouse and William Smyth of Hill, tenants of the Queen, two messuages, other buildings, and 21 acres 1 rood of land in Brereclif and lately in the tenure of Thomas Glov' and Brian Glover, deceased, to the use of John Woodrof, junior, Edmund Robinson of Oldlande and Edmund Tattersall, son of the said Richard Tattersall, and their heirs as feofees according to an indenture made by (1) the said Robert Glov' and (2) Brian Clowdisley of Hallton aforesaid, yeoman, dated 12th June 6 Elizabeth I [1564]. Admittance sought and granted. Fine 7s 1d by the pledge of William Follds.

Richard Ingham of Bruneleywood surrendered one close of land called le croftes containing 2 acres of land and also two houses built thereon in Bruneleywood, in the tenure of John Ingham or his assigns, to George Tattersall and his assigns for five years from 15th May 1570 according to the intent. Admittance sought and granted. Fine 8d by the pledge of Lawrence Whitacar.

The intent was that George Tattersall was to be seised of the property to the use of himself and his assigns for five years from 15th April [sic] 1570. Provided always that if the said Richard Ingham, his heirs, executors or assigns paid to the said George Tatt'sall, his executors or assigns £4 12s on 2nd July 1569 then this surrender was to be void.

At the halmote of the manor aforesaid held on Thursday, 4th December, 10 Elizabeth I [1567] it was presented that one messuage and other buildings in Bruneley, in the tenure of Nicholas Sager, came into the Queen's hands by the death of Richard Whithead. John Whitehead was his son and next heir and of full age. Admittance sought and granted. Fine 1d by the pledge of Hugh Hallstead, gent.

At the halmote of the manor aforesaid held on Thursday, 4th December, 10 Elizabeth I [1567] it was presented that one messuage and other buildings and 3½ acres 1 rood of land in Bruneleywoode, in the tenure of Richard Mitchell, came into the Queen's hands by the death of Margaret Hallsted, lately wife of William Hallstead of le Banckhouse. Henry Hallstead was her son and next heir and aged about fifteen and [blank] was his guardian. Admittance sought and granted. Fine 15d by the pledge of Francis Webster.

John Woodrof, junior, Edmund Robinson of Oldlaunde, and Edmund, son of Richard Tattersall of Rige, at the request of Thomas Glov' of Hallton de le Hill in Craven in the county of York, surrendered two messuages, other buildings and 21 acres 1 rood of land in Brereclif within the jurisdiction of this court, lately in the tenure of Thomas Glover and Brian Glover, deceased, to Bernard Towneley of Hurstwood, gent., and John Woodrof, senior, and their heirs, for ever as feofees according to an indenture made by (1) the said Thomas Glover of Hallton and (2) the said Richard Tattersall dated 22nd April 8 Elizabeth I [1566]. Admittance sought and granted. Fine 7s 1d by the pledge of Hugh Hallstead, gent.

Sum of this halmote £8 10s ½d approved.

[Membrane 7]

Bruneley
Halmote of the manor of Ightenhill held at Bruneley, Monday, 11th July, 11 Elizabeth I [1569] before John Towneley, esq., chief steward there.

Inquisition taken there for the Queen to make enquiry upon the oaths of Hugh Hallstead, gent., John Houghton, John Whitacar of Micklehurste, Robert Whitacar of Healey, Robert Ingham, James Foldes, Richard Tattersall, Richard Acroyde, Robert Brereclif, George Smythe, John Higgyn, Robert Towne, Nicholas Hargreaves, Robert Houghton and William Lund, senior.

Richard Dicconson, Richard Heigh and John Ingham of Lone were elected greaves of Ightenhill of the Old Hold.

John Watmough (2s) because he kept illegal games in his house contrary to the statute.

Edmund Leigh (2d) and William Boith (2d) because they dug and got turfs for fuel for the fire contrary to the bye-laws.

James Whithead (12d) because he revealed the deliberations of the jurors in public.

Richard Whitacar of Micklehurst (4d) and Richard Tattersall (4d) because they made a rescue upon Richard Ingham and James Whithead, pounders for Bruneley More.

Robert Whitacar of Healey (12d) because he broke the Queen's fold.

Nicholas Hauworth (2d), Richard Whitacar (2d), Richard Tattersall (2d), George Tattersall (2d), John Withington (2d), James Pillinge (4d), John Yate (4d), Miles Ingham (4d) because they trespassed on the common pasture of Bruneley.

Thomas Whitacar of Symondston (12d) because he made an affray upon Leonard Cronckeshay.

Hugh More of le Deane (12d) because he broke the Queen's fold in Padih'm.

Thomas Jackeson (2d), Richard Ingham (2d), Lawrence Leaver (2d), Benedict[?] Lee (2d), Nicholas Folldes Foldes [*sic*] (2d) and Thomas Folldes (2d) because they trespassed upon Bruneley More with their livestock.

A penalty of 20s was imposed at the last halmote that Anne Towneley, widow, lately wife of Nicholas Towneley, esq., deceased, should lay open one usual and ancient way upon and through her land and tenement called le Roylhill before the date of this halmote which she refused to do and so far had not done. Therefore she was in mercy.

Amercements 29s 10d.

Richard Tattersall, a tenant of the Queen, surrendered one messuage, one garden containing one hundred feet in length and sixty feet in width in Bruneley, in the tenure of the relict of Richard Willson, (which Christopher Aspeden and Margery, his wife, delivered to him) to Margaret Blakey, widow, and her heirs for ever. Admittance sought and granted. Fine 1d by the pledge of John Blakey.

John Webster of Padih'm surrendered by John Houghton, a tenant of the Queen, one close of land called le Carr or Eyes containing 2 acres of land in the west part of Padiham, to Thomas Londisdale of Symondston and his assigns for the life of the said John Webster. Admittance sought and granted. Fine 8d by the pledge of the said John Houghtoms [*sic*].

John Webster of Padiham surrendered by Robert Houghton, a tenant of the Queen, 3 acres of land in the west part of Padih'm, in the tenure of Edmund Starkye, gent., and his assigns, and also remised and granted all title, interest and claim which he had, formerly had or should have in future of and in the 3 acres to the said Edmund Starky and his assigns for the life of the said John Webster. Admittance sought and granted. Fine 12d by the pledge of Robert Roo.

Bernard Towneley, gent., and John Woodrof, feofees of Richard Tattersall of Ridge, at the request of the said Richard, surrendered one messuage, other buildings and 10½ acres ½ a rood of land, in the tenure of John Hanson als. Bent, in Brereclif within the jurisdiction of this court, to the said John Hanson als. Bent and his assigns for life. Admittance sought and granted. An annual rent of 13s 4d was payable to Robert Glov' and Thomas Glov' and their heirs and assigns during the said term. Fine 3s 6¼d by the pledge of Hugh Hallstead.

Bernard Towneley, gent., and John Woodroff of Bruneley, senior, feofees of Richard Tattersall of Rige, at the request of the said Richard, surrendered one messuage, other buildings and 10½ acres ½ a rood of land in Brerecliff, in the tenure of Thomas Glov' of Cockeden, to Evan Haydock, gent., and George Smythe of Hollyngreave, their heirs and assigns, as feofees according to the intent. Admittance sought and granted. Fine 3s 6¼d by the pledge of Hugh Hallstead.

The intent was that the feofees were to be seised of the property for twenty years from the feast of St. Martin the Bishop in Winter next [11th November], to Alexander Gryme and his assigns, he the said Alexander paying not only the rent and service due to the Queen, her heirs and successors, but also the yearly rent of 13s 4d to one Robert Glov' and Thomas Glov'. Provided always that if the above named Richard Tattersall could otherwise provide for the said Alexander according to his contention and as should be thought reasonable by John Townley, esq., Richard Smythez and 'Ewyne' Haydock, gentlemen, that then the said Alexander should resurrender the premises to the said Richard Tattersall.

Robert, son and heir of John Hallsted of Highehallsted, surrendered by John Towneley, esq., chief steward there, one messuage, other buildings and 16 acres of land, meadow, grazing and pasture in Brereclif, in the tenure of the said John Hallsted or his assigns, to John Parker of Wurstorne and his assigns for twenty years after the death of the said John Hallsted of Highehallsted. That is to say according to an indenture made by (1) the said Robert Hallsted and John, his son, and (2) the said John Parker dated 8th October 9 Elizabeth I [1567]. Admittance sought. The said John Halsted forbade fine in the name of Hugh Halsted as the said Hugh had the premises for the life of James Sager. John Parker found pledge Nicholas Haworth to answer the forbid and admittance was then granted. Fine 5s 4d by the pledge aforesaid.

Sum of this halmote 43s 11½d approved.

Sum of the two halmotes of Ightenhill aforesaid £10 14s
Fines for land £7 16 5d; amercements 57s 7d
Approved and charged in the 11th year of Queen Elizabeth.
[*Membrane 7d*]

Tottington
Halmote of the manor of Tottington held at Hollcome, Tuesday, 14th December, 11 Elizabeth I [1568] before John Towneley, esq., chief steward there.

Inquisition taken there for the Queen to make enquiry upon the oaths of Lawrence Rawstorne, gent., James Assheworth, John Cowopp, Edmund Lawe, Henry

Cowopp, Richard Romesbothome, Richard Roithewell, Ralph Bridge, Charles Nuttowe, John Hollte, Thomas Wood, Thomas Grenehaulgh, Thurstan Hamer, Richard Boithe and Thomas Roithewell.

William Burye was elected greave of Tottington; Lawrence Rawstorne, gent., and Richard Romesbothome were elected affeerors; John Hollt and Thurstan Hamer were elected constables; Ralph Bridge and Henry Cowoopp were elected fence lookers; Thomas Wood and John Cowoop were elected appraisers for the Queen; Thomas Nabbs and John Cowoop, junior, were elected pounders; Edmund Lawe and James Assheworth were elected moss lookers; Richard Rawstorne and Richard Boith were elected aletasters.

Richard Tailior, miller, (12d) because he kept and used illegal measures to the harm of the poor people.
Thomas Nabbs, senior, (8d) did likewise.
Geoffrey Hauworth (8d) because he trespassed with his livestock in Alden.
John Leache (12d) because he stopped up a usual way to the Queen's mill.
Amercements 3s 4d.

Edward, Lord Derby, judge of Bury; the heir of Richard Assheton, esq., under age, judge of Midleton; the heir of Robert Langley, knight, judge of Alcrington; and Edmund Assheton, esq., judge of Chatt'ton & Foxdenton, appeared in court by their attornies.[1]
The constables of Bury, Mydleton, Alcrington, and Chatt'ton and Foxdento' appeared in court.

Fee of Tottington
Inquisition taken there for the Queen to make enquiry upon the oaths of Roger Ogden, John Gryme, John Heald, Henry Smethurste, John As'mall, John Horrockes, John Ellens, Richard Kirkema', William Ogden, Thomas Radclif, Alexander Neild, Thomas Scoles and Henry Buckeley.

Robert Levesey (3s 4d) and William Duckeworth (3s 4d) because they made an affray and drew blood upon Arthur Smethurste.
Edmund Holt (6s 8d) and his son because they made an affray and drew blood upon Arthur Holt and his son.
Sum of this halmote 16s 8d.

---

[1] Bury, Middleton, Alkrington and Chatterton and Foxdenton, together with the manor of Tottington itself, made up the Fee of Tottington. Since the first four manors were dependants of the latter, their lords owed suit at the Tottington halmote.

Tottington
Halmote of the manor of Tottington held at Hollcome, Saturday, 18th June, 11 Elizabeth I [1569] before John Towneley, esq., chief steward there.

Inquisition taken there for the Queen to make enquiry upon the oaths of Lawrence Rawstorne, gent., Charles Nuttowe, gent., John Hollte, Richard Rawstorne, Richard Romesbothome, Richard Boithe, James Assheworth, John Cowopp, Henry Cowopp, senior, Thomas Wood, Thomas Grenehaulgh, Ralph Bridge, Richard Roithewell, Thurstan Hamer, Ralph Hauworthe and Thomas Roithewell.

Robert Shipplebothom (3s 4d) and John Roithwell (20d) because they made an affray together.
John Broke (3s 4d) because he made an affray upon Thomas Bridge.
Ralph Bridge of Burch Heigh (12d) because he did not mill or grind his corn and grain at the Queen's mill.
Richard Romesbothome (12d) because he overstocked the common pasture in Tottington.
Richard Nuttowe (12d) and Ralph Bury (12d) did likewise.
Amercements 12s 4d.

Edward, Lord Derby, judge of Bury; the heir of Richard Assheton, esq., under age, judge of Midleton; the heir of Robert Langley, knight, judge of Alcrington; and Edmund Assheton, esq., judge of Chatt'ton and Foxdenton, appeared in court by their attornies.
The constables of Bury, Mydleton, Alcrington, and Chatt'ton and Foxdenton appeared in court.

Fee of Tottington
Inquisition taken there for the Queen to make enquiry upon the oaths of Francis Grenehaulgh, Roger Kaye of Shipplebothome, John Wood, Roger Kay of Elton, Thomas Levesey, Edmund Hewhard, Geoffrey Lomasse, William Ogden, Thomas Radclif, Henry Buckeley, Richard Waward, Richard Hall and James Ogden.

The jury had nothing to present because all was well.

To this halmote, by virtue of a certain decree made by the Chancellor and Council of the Duchy of Lancaster in the Duchy Chamber in the Michaelmas term, namely Thursday, 7th November, 8 Elizabeth I [1566] between John Anysworth, plaintiff, and Richard Morres, defendant, thus enrolled in the court, Thomas Anysworth of Blacklawe, now deceased, on 16th June 1564 and the first year of the reign of Mary, Queen of England, outside the court according to the custom of the manor, surrendered by Thomas Grenhaulgh, greave of the manor, in the presence of

Ralph Nuttall, Charles Nuttall, junior, Oliver Lawe, Lawrence Tailior, Bartholomew Grenhaulgh, William Lumas and others, one messuage, 59 acres 3 roods of land called Blacklawe, Redisher and Bathfeilde in Tottington within the jurisdiction of this court with their appurtenances in Tottington and Alden, to Richard Romesbothome and Thomas Woode, now living, and John Grenehaulgh and Francis Warberton, now dead, and their heirs with this intention that the said Richard, Thomas, John and Francis and their heirs should be seised to the use of John Ainsworth, kinsman of the said Thomas Ainsworth, namely son of James Ainsworth, the son of the said Thomas, and his heirs for ever. The surrender was presented to the next court by the greave. The feofees could not be admitted because a certain Giles Morres and Agnes, his wife, in the right of the same Agnes, forbade them from being admitted. They alleged that Agnes was the kinswoman and heiress of the said Thomas Ainsworth, namely she was the daughter and heiress of a certain Henry Ainsworth, son and heir apparent whilst he lived of the said Thomas Ainsworth, and that the said Thomas was lunatic at the time of the surrender and was compelled to make the surrender by force of arms. After the death of the said Thomas Ainsworth, Giles and Agnes got the seisin for themselves as of Agnes's right as the kinswoman and heiress of the said Thomas Ainsworth. And afterwards this aforesaid business was aired both between the said Giles and Agnes, plaintiffs, and the said John Ainsworth, defendant, and also, after the deaths of Giles and Agnes, between the said John Ainsworth, plaintiff, and Richard Morres, son and heir of the said Agnes, defendant, before the Chancellor and Council of the Duchy of Lancaster in the same Duchy's Chamber at Westminster. The legal process was continued there between the parties until 7th November in the eighth year of the reign of the present queen, namely 1566, on which day it was decreed by the said Chancellor and Council of the said Duchy for the same John Ainsworth, just as appears more fully by the same decree under the seal of the Duchy, shown by the said steward and remaining in the custody of the said John Ainsworth. And upon this, the Queen, by her steward, at the petition of the said Richard Romesbothom and Thomas Wood, according to the tenor of the same decree, granted to the said Richard and Thomas seisin in the messuage, 59 acres 3 roods of land with appurtenances, which Thomas Ainsworth had formerly surrendered outside the court, as was said before, to hold the property to themselves and their heirs and assigns according to the custom of the manor. Richard Morres forbade fine by right of his inheritance and Richard Romesbothom and Thomas Wood were admitted according to the intent of the surrender made by the said Thomas Ainsworth. Fine 20s.

Afterwards the said Richard Romesbothome and Thomas Woode surrendered the property to the said John Ainsworth for ever. Admittance sought. Richard Morres forbade fine by right of his inheritance. John Ainsworth was then admitted. Fine 20s by the pledge of William Brooke.

Sum of this halmote 56s 4d.

Sum of the two halmotes of Todington 79s
Greave; 55s 8d; fines for land 40s, amercements, 15s 8d.
Bailiff; 17s 4d, total of amercements.
Approved and charged in the 10th year of Queen Elizabeth.

COURT ROLL OF THE HONOR OF CLITHEROE
MICHAELMAS 1569 - EASTER 1570

[Membrane 1]

Chatburne
**Halmote of the manors of Chatburne, Wurston and Penhulton held at
Clitherowe Castle, Tuesday, 10th January, 12 Elizabeth I [1569/70], before
John Towneley, esq., chief steward there.**

Inquisition taken there for the Queen to make enquiry upon the oaths of Thomas
Robynson, Thomas Tailior, James Harropp, John Dugdale of Le Scarr, John Hirde,
William Heiryson, Edmund Dawson, Richard Mersden, John Wulton, James
Altham, Geoffrey Kendale, John Dawson and Richard Dugdale.

Christopher Corbrigge was elected greave of Chatburne; John Dugdale, senior,
and John Tailior, webster, were elected constables of Chatburne; Richard
Grenacers, gent., was elected greave of Wurston; James Browne was elected
constable of Wurston; John Smythe was elected greave of Penhulton; and Francis
Webster and John Moore were elected constables of Penhulto'.

Margaret Hirde surrendered by Thomas Nowell, greave of Chatburne, 3 acres of
land in Bradfurthbrigstede, Stielfurth, Shotland, Stielfurthbancke and Hall Inge
within the manor of Chatburne, of the 'halldemayne' land, in the tenure of William
Tailior, to the said William and his heirs as feofees according to the intent.
Admittance sought. John Tailior forbade fine by Nicholas Hyrde by right of his
inheritance. William Tailior found pledge Thomas Tailor to answer the forbid and
admittance was then granted. Fine 12d by the pledge aforesaid.
    The intent was that William Tailior and his heirs should be seised of the property
to the use of the said William Tailior and Margaret Hirde for life. And after their
deaths to the use of their lawfully begotten heirs, and in default of such issue then
to the use of the right heirs of the said William for ever.

Nicholas Robinson surrendered by Thomas Tailior, a tenant of the Queen, three messuages, three tofts and 26 acres of oxgang land in Chatborn. Also 21½ acres ½ a rood of rodeland in Chatburne. And also 14 acres of land called le Halldemayne in Chatburne, to Thomas Robynson, son and heir apparent of the said Nicholas, and his heirs for ever. Admittance sought. Agnes, wife of the said Nicholas, forbade fine for her dower. Thomas Robinson found pledges Richard Kendall, senior, and William Harryson, to answer the forbid. Admittance was then granted. Fine 20s 6d.

Thomas Robinson, feofee, at the request of Richard Kendale, senior, and Agnes, his wife, surrendered one messuage, one garden, half of one barn with one oxgang of oxgang land in Chatburne, in the tenure of the said Richard Kendale and his assigns, to Richard Kendale, son of the said Richard and Agnes, and his heirs for ever. Admittance sought. Richard Kendale, the father, and Agnes, his wife, forbade fine as they held the premises for themselves and their assigns for life. James Harropp forbade fine by an agreement made with him by the said Richard Kendall, the father, at the time of his marriage. Richard Kendale, the son, found pledge William Smythez to answer James Harropp's forbid and granted in open court that his parents were to have all the premises during their lives. Admittance was then granted. Fine 3s by the pledge aforesaid.

Sum of this court 24s 6d.

Chatburne
Halmote of the manors of Chatburne, Wurston and Penhulton held at Clitherowe Castle, Thursday, 27th July, 12 Elizabeth I [1570] before John Towneley, esq., chief steward there.

Inquisition taken there for the Queen to make enquiry upon the oaths of Thomas Robinson, Richard Kendale, senior, Edmund Dawson, Thomas Tailior, William Harryson, John Hirde, James Harropp, Geoffrey Kendale, Richard Dugdale, John Dawson, Christopher Midgecock, John Moore, Ottiwell Feilden, James Altham and John Atkinson.

Chatburn
Thomas Chatburne (2d) because he overstocked le Cowpastur with his horses contrary to the bye-laws.

John Corbridge (2d) and Richard Tailier (2d) because they cut down 'hollyns' in le Cowpasture contrary to the bye-laws.

Thomas Fenton (6d) because he often kept his mare in le Cowpastur contrary to the bye-laws.

Adam Smythe (excused) and Thomas Hodgeson (4d) because they did not do suit at the court aforesaid.

Christopher Hargreaves (2d) because he overstocked le Cowpastur with a certain cow contrary to the bye-laws.

Amercements 18d.

Wurston

William Hurste (4d) because he did not do suit at the said court.
Roger Nowell, gent., (6d) for not doing likewise.

Amercements 10d.

Ralph Whithed, Master of Arts, Thomas Tailior, Thomas Hirde and Richard Radclyf, lately feofees of Thomas Chatburne, deceased, at the request of Thomas Chatburne, junior, surrendered by John Dugdale, senior, a tenant of the Queen, one house, one garden, 1½ acres of rodeland in Chatburne and 4½ acres of oxgang land in Chatburne, in the tenure of Thomas Chatburne, junior, and his assigns, to the said Thomas and his heirs for ever. Admittance sought and granted. Fine 2s by the pledge of Richard Kendale, senior.

Sum of this court 4s 4d.

Sum of the two aforesaid halmotes 28s 10d
Chatburne 26s, fines for land 24s 6d, amercements 18d; Wurston 2s 10d, fines for land 2s, amercements 10d; Penhulton nothing.
Approved and charged in the 12th year of Queen Elizabeth.

[Membrane 1d]

Halmote of the manor of Acryngton held there Friday, 4th November, 11 Elizabeth I [1569] before John Towneley, esq., chief steward there.

Inquisition taken there of the Old Hold for the Queen to make enquiry upon the oaths of Francis Garsid, gent., Robert Dureden, Richard Dureden, Robert Gregory, Richard Roithwell, James Roithewell, Richard Hargreaves, junior, Christopher Jackson, Giles Whitacar, John Ormerod, Richard Aithalghe, Henry Ryley, Lawrence Jackson, John Ryddinge and John Ryley.

Adam Holden, gent., was elected greave of Haslingden; Ralph Tailior was elected constable of Haslingden; Thomas Garside and John Radclif, junior, were elected appraisers; Hugh Tailior and Giles Roithewell were elected fence lookers; John Whitacar was elected greave of Accrington and Huncot; James Yate was elected constable there and Richard Aithaulghe and John Ryley were elected appraisers and fence lookers.

Accrington Old Hold

Gilbert Russheton surrendered by John Kenyon and Thomas Riley, tenants of the Queen, 5 acres of land in Oswaldtwisill, in the tenure of John Ianson, to Robert

Russheton, son of the said Gilbert, and his heirs for ever. Admittance sought. Ralph Ianson forbade fine for the said John Ianson and Lettice, his wife, and for himself for their lives. James Crosley forbade fine for ½ an acre, a parcel of the premises, by right of his inheritance. Robert Russheton found pledge John Nuttall to answer the forbids and admittance was then granted. Fine 20d by the pledge aforesaid.

John Birtwisill surrendered by Thomas Ryley and Christopher Jackson, tenants of the Queen, one messuage, other buildings, and 20 acres ½ a rood of land in Huncote within the jurisdiction of this court, to George Birtwisill and Alice, his wife, for their lives. Admittance sought. Oliver Birtwisill, gent., forbade fine for a certain encroachment. George and Alice found pledge Thomas Ryley to answer the forbid and admittance was then granted. Fine 6s 8d by the pledge aforesaid.

Forest of Rossindale
Inquisition taken there of the Forest for the Queen to make enquiry upon the oaths of Lawrence Nuttall, John Ormerod, senior, George Dureden, Oliver Pillinge, Dionysius Hauworth, junior, Francis Bridge of Musbury, John Piccopp, Christopher Brige of Dedwencloughe, Richard Crawshaie, Hugh Pillinge, John Lord als. Bolton, Ralph Nuttall, James Piccopp of Wullfinden, Christopher Hargreaves, Ellis Cunlyf, Henry Hollden, Lawrence Holden, Ambrose Russheton, James Wallmersley and Robert Hauworthe.

Henry Hauworth was elected greave of Rossindale; Christopher Hargreaves was elected greave of Accrington New Hold.

Robert Romesden (2d) and William Brigge (2d) because they carried away turfs without right from Richard Rawstorne's moss.

John Pillinge (8d) because he kept his fences open to the damage of his neighbours.

John Hauworth of Yate (2d) because he turned a water course in Crawshaybothe between his land and tenement and the land and tenement of Edward Romesbothome from its right course into a contrary one.

Ralph Duckworth (12d) because he turned a water course in Musbury between his land and tenement and the land and tenement of Thomas Duckworth from its right course into a contrary one.
Amercements 2s 2d.

Dionysius Hauworth, greave of Rossindale, surrendered one messuage, other buildings, lands, tenements, meadows, grazing lands, pastures, moors and mosses in Goodshaieboth and Henherds, annual rent to the Queen 13s 6½d ¼d, which Thurstan Birtwisill delivered to him, to John Birtwisill and his heirs as feofees according to the intent. Admittance sought and granted. Fine 13s 6½d ¼d by the pledge of George Hargreaves.

The intent was that John Birtwisill and his heirs were to be seised of the property to the use of the said Thurstan Birtwisill for life, and after his death, to the use of Margaret, wife of the said Thurstan, during her widowhood if she survived him.

Peter Ormerod of Ormerod and Oliver Ormerod of Crawshaieboth (at the request of George Ormerod of Gambleside), surrendered by Dionysius Hauworth, greave of Rossindale, the fourth part of one messuage and other buildings, lands, tenements, meadows, grazing lands and pastures in Gamblesid and Wullfinden in the Forest of Rossindale, annual rent to the Queen 28s 1d, to Henry, son of George Hergreaves, Adam, son of Edmund Romesbothome, Bernard Towneley of Hurstwood, Ellis Nutter [Cunlyf *crossed out*] of Rydihalowes and their heirs as feofees according to the intent. Admittance sought. James Birtwisill forbade fine by the right of the inheritance of Agnes, his wife. Henry Hargreaves and his co-feofees found pledge John Nuttall to answer the forbid and admittance was then granted. Fine 7s¼d by the pledge aforesaid.

The intent was that Henry Hargreaves and his co-feofees were to be seised of the property to the use of such woman as should be the wife of the said George Ormerod at the day of his death for her life as her jointure and dower.

Dionysius Hauworth, greave of Rossindale, surrendered one messuage, other buildings, lands, tenements, meadows, grazing lands, pastures and mosses in Woulfenden in the Forest of Rossindale, annual rent to the Queen 12s 8d, in the tenure of Robert Ferror of Briggeroid in the county of York, clothier, Roger Schofeld and Lawrence Assheworth, which premises the said Robert Ferror delivered to him, to John Hargreaves and his heirs for ever. Admittance sought. Roger Schofeild forbade fine as he had half of the premises for himself and Isabel, his wife, for their lives. The same was granted by John Hargreaves in open court and he was then admitted. Fine 12s 8d by the pledge of George Dureden.

[*The following note is added in English.*] Provided always and where it is granted by John Hargreaves that Roger Scofeld and Isabel, his wife, upon a forbid in the said surrender entered should have the half of the lands, tenements and hereditaments during their lives, the true meaning of the surrender, notwithstanding the same grant, is that Isabel, if she happens to survive Roger, shall after his decease have but the fourth part of the same lands for life.

[Membrane 2]

Francis Nuttall surrendered by Dionysius Hauworth, greave of Rossindale, half of one messuage, other buildings, and one parcel of land, meadow, grazing land and pasture in Cowopp in the Forest of Rossindale called le Cowopp cragghead, annual rent to the Queen 12d, in the tenure of Gilbert Hill, to John Nuttall of Newalheigh and his assigns from the feast of the Purification of the Blessed Virgin Mary [2nd February] next after this halmote for twenty-four years. Admittance sought and granted. Fine 12d by the pledge of Bernard Towneley.

John Tattersall of Tunstede, senior, surrendered by John Nuttall, a tenant of the Queen, one messuage, other buildings, and a parcel of land, meadow, grazing land and pasture in Tunsted, Sedges and Soweclough in the Forest of Rossindale, annual rent to the Queen 28s, in the tenure of the said John Tattersall and John Tattersall, his son, to John the son, his heirs and assigns as feofees according to the intent. Admittance sought. Gilbert Lawe forbade fine as he had a way through the land and tenement. John Tattersall the son found pledge John Nuttall to answer the forbid and admittance was then granted. Fine 28s by the pledge aforesaid.

The intent was that John Tatt'sall the younger and his heirs were to be seised of the property to the use of John Tattersall the older for his life. And after his death, to be seised of two parts of the property (the whole being divided into three parts) to the use of Alice, wife of John the older, and her assigns for eight years for the bringing up of her children. At the end of the eight years, the feofee was to be seised to the use of the said Alice for all of her 'puer wydowhod', she paying yearly at the feast of [blank] only to Jennet, daughter of John Tattersall the older, the sum of 8s. If she married another man after her husband's death, then from thenceforth John Tattersall the younger and his heirs were to be seised of only half of the two parts to the use of the said Alice and her assigns for life. The remainder of all the premises to the use of the said John Tattersall, the son, his heirs and assigns for ever.

John Tattersall of Tunsted, junior, surrendered by John Nuttall, a tenant of the Queen, one messuage, other buildings, lands, tenements, meadows, grazing lands and pastures in Wullfinden in the Forest of Rossindale called le Shawclough, annual rent to the Queen 5s 4d, in the tenure of the said John Tattersall and John Tattersall, his father, to George Tattersall, his brother, and his assigns for life. Admittance sought and granted. Fine 5s 4d by the pledge of John Nuttall.

Thomas Piccopp surrendered one messuage, other buildings, and one parcel of land in Rawtonstall in the Forest of Rossindale, annual rent to the Queen 1d, in the tenure of Oliver Piccopp, to Lawrence Rawstorne, gent., and Edward Rawstorne, his son, and their heirs for ever. Admittance sought and granted. Fine 1d by the pledge of John Nuttowe.

Haslingden
Richard Dureden surrendered by Adam Holden, greave of Haslingden, two messuages, other buildings, and 36½ acres of land in Haslingden, to Richard, son of the said Richard Dureden, and his heirs for ever. Admittance sought. Richard Dureden the father forbade fine not only as he had all the premises for himself and his heirs for life but also so that he might have sufficient dower for his wife at the time of his death. This was granted to him in open court and he was then admitted. Fine 12s 12d by the pledge of Adam Hollden, gent.

Sum of this court, £4 11s 3d.

[*Membrane 2d*]

Accrington

Halmote of the manor of Accrington held there Friday, 26th May, 12 Elizabeth I [1570] before John Towneley, esq., chief steward there.

Inquisition taken there for the Queen to make enquiry upon the oaths of Francis Garside, gent., John Nuttall, Robert Dureden, Richard Dureden, Robert Gregory, Robert Heigh, John Heapp, junior, Richard Roithwell, junior, John Kenyon, Henry Ryley, Giles Whitacar, Christopher Jackeson, Percival Grymeshawe, William Collinson and John Ormerod.

Haslingden

Thomas Tailior (12d) and Roger Jackeson (*erased*) because they made an affray together.

Robert Gregory (6d) and Richard Tailior (6d) because they made an affray together.

Amercements 2s.

Haslingden

Hugh Garside of Ewood surrendered by Richard Smythes, gent., deputy steward of Blagburneshier, 2 acres of land in Haslingden adjacent to the lower part of John Nuttall's land, in the tenure of James Jackson, to the said John Nuttall and his heirs for ever. Admittance sought and granted. Fine 8d by the pledge of John Kenyon.

James Hartley and Jennet, his wife, surrendered by Adam Holden, greave of Haslingden, one messuage, other buildings, and the fifth part of le Stryndes accordingly as the same is now enclosed, containing 7½ acres and the fifth part of 1 acre of land in Haslingden, in the tenure of James Hartley and Adam Roithwell, to Lawrence Rawstorne, gent., and Edward, his son, and their heirs for ever. Admittance sought and granted. Fine 2s 6d by the pledge of John Nuttall.

Forest of Rossindale

Inquisition taken there of the Forest for the Queen to make enquiry upon the oaths of Lawrence Nuttall, John Ormerod of Gambleside, senior, Gilbert Birtwisill, Oliver Pillinge, Dionysius Hauworth of Crawshaieboth, junior, Dionysius Hauworth of Constableleigh, Christopher Bridge of Dedwenclough, George Nuttall, John Lord als. Bolton, Hugh Pillinge of Tunsted, Ralph Hauworth of Musbury, Nicholas Russheton, Christopher Hargreaves, Ellis Cunlyf and James Gryme.

Henry Heape (4d), Jennet, his wife, and Roger Nuttall (2d) because they made a rescue on the greave of Rossindall while he was carrying out his office.

John Lawe (8d) because he kept his fences open between the land of Robert Lord and the land of John Lord als. Bolton and Tunsted [*sic*].

Amercements 14d.

Edmund Assheworth died about the date of the last court seised of one messuage and a parcel of land called Cotebank dole in the Forest of Rossindale, annual rent to the Queen 12d. James Assheworth was his son and next heir and aged about eight and Edmund Pillinge was his guardian. Admittance sought and granted. Fine 12d by the pledge of Christopher Nuttall.

Christopher, son of John Hollgate, Hugh Heigh, and Jennet, his wife, surrendered by George Hargreaves and Gilbert Birtwisill, tenants of the Queen, one messuage, other buildings, and one parcel of land called Wetehead in Wullfinden, Henhedes and Frerehill in the Forest of Rossindale, annual rent to the Queen 2s, to John Piccopp and Gilbert Heighe and their heirs as feofees according to the intent. Admittance sought and granted. Fine 4s by the pledge of Richard Crawshawe.

The intent was that John Pyccopp and Gilbert Heghe and their heirs were to be seised of the property to the use of Hugh Heigh and Jennet, his wife, for their lives. After their deaths to the use of Robert, son and heir of the said Hugh Heighe, and his heirs for ever. Provided always that if the said Robert Heigh, his heirs, executors or assigns did not pay to Richard, oldest son of the said Hugh Heighe, or his assigns at the day of the death of the said Hugh Heigh and Jennet, his wife, or at the day of the death of the survivor of them, or within forty days then next following, the sum of £8 10s at the said Hugh Heigh's dwelling house in Rowtonstall, then the feofees and their heirs should thenceforth be seised of the property to the use of the said Richard Heighe, his heirs and assigns for ever.

[Membrane 3]

John Nuttall of Newalheigh surrendered one parcel of the pasture of Henhead in the Forest of Rossindale, annual rent to the Queen 1d, in the tenure of John Kenyon of Accrington, which he lately bought from Oliver Pyccopp, to the said John Kenyon and his heirs for ever. Admittance sought and granted. Fine 1d by the pledge of Lawrence Nuttall.

John Nuttall of Newalheigh surrendered by Lawrence Rawstorne, gent., greave of Rossindall, four closes of land in Newalheigh called Lower Warth, Lower Heighes, Little Water Bank and Great Water Bank, in the Forest of Rossindale, annual rent to the Queen 10s, to Elizabeth, daughter of John Ormerod, and her assigns from the death of Christopher, son of the said John Nuttall, for life. Admittance sought and granted. Fine 10s by the pledge of Lawrence Nuttall.

Dionysius Hauworth of Crawshaieboth, junior, surrendered by Lawrence Nuttall, a tenant of the Queen, half of one house called 'a berne' and half of a parcel of land in Wullfinden, annual rent to the Queen 4s 4d, all in the Forest of Rossindale, to John Romesden and his assigns from the feast of the Annunciation of the Blessed Virgin Mary [25th March] last for twenty-one years. Admittance sought and granted. Fine 4s 4d by the pledge of John Lord.

At the halmote of the manor of Accrington held there on Monday, 22nd December, 10 Elizabeth I [1567] before the said steward, it was presented that

William Yate, senior, died seised of one messuage, other buildings, and certain parcels of land in Hodlesden in the Forest of Rossindale, annual rent to the Queen 11s 11¼d. George Yate was his son and next heir and aged about eighteen and William Tomlynson was his guardian. Admittance sought. Ellen Yate, widow, forbade fine for her dower and the same was granted to her in open court. Admittance was then granted. Fine 11s 11¼d by the pledge of William Yate.

At the halmote of the manor of Accrington held there on Tuesday, 1st June, 10 Elizabeth I [1568] before the steward aforesaid, it was presented that Grace, lately wife of John Ormerode, deceased, died seised of certain messuages, other buildings, and certain parcels of land in Bacoppboithe als. Horelawehead and Wullfinden in the Forest of Rossindale, annual rent to the Queen 5s 1d and the third part of 1d, in the tenure of Christopher Bridge. Jennet, wife of John Lord als. Bolton, Katherine, wife of John Lord son of Jenken, Alice, wife of Thomas Robt'shaie, and Isabel Robt'shaie, widow, were sisters of the said Grace and her next heirs and were of full age. Admittance sought and granted. Fine 5s 1d and the third part of 1d by the pledge of John Nuttowe.

Release

Afterwards at the same halmote John Ormerode of Huncote surrendered the property and quitclaimed for himself and his heirs all right, estate, interest and demand which they had, or should have had in future in the property, to the said Jennet, wife of John Lord als. Bolton, Katherine, wife of John Lord als. Jenken, Alice, wife of Thomas Robt'shaie and Isabel Robt'shaie, widow, and their heirs for ever. Admittance sought and granted. Fine [*blank*] by the pledge of John Nuttowe.

Haslingden

At the halmote of the manor of Accrington held there, Tuesday, 1st June, 10 Elizabeth I [1568] before the steward aforesaid, it was presented that Lawrence Fenton died seised of three messuages, other buildings, and 5 acres of land in Rossindale and Haslingden. Lawrence Fenton was his son and next heir and was aged about one year and Richard Jackeson was his guardian. Lawrence the son sought admittance. Hugh Fenton forbade fine by the right of Margaret, his wife, as he had all the premises for her life and after her death should have half of the premises for life. The said Hugh Fenton also forbade fine in the name of two children lawfully begotten of his body and to be nominated by him during his lifetime to have two houses now in the tenure of Lawrence Fenton, senior, and Sybil, lately wife of Lawrence Fenton, junior, deceased, for the lives of the said two children. Paying to Lawrence Fenton, the son, and his heirs 4d at the usual feast days annually during their lives. Lawrence Fenton the son found pledge Adam Holden to answer the forbids. Admittance was then granted. Fine 10d by the pledge aforesaid.

Huncote. Accrington Old [Hold *omitted*]

Henry Cowoopp of Olerbothome surrendered one messuage, other buildings, and 12½ acres of land in Huncote within the jurisdiction of this court, to John

Brandwood of Padiham and Lawrence, son of Lawrence Brandwood of Altham, and their heirs as feofees according to the intent. Admittance sought and granted. Fine 8s 2d by the pledge of John Nuttowe.

[*In English*] Memorandum that Thomas Whitacar forbade the fine for the dower of Elizabeth, now wife of the said Henry Cowopp, and John Nutow.

The intent was that John and Lawrence Brandwood were to be seised of the property to the use of Roger Cowopp of Huncote for life, he yielding and paying not only to the Queen and her heirs and successors the rent and service due and of right accustomed, but also to the said Henry Cowopp, his heirs and assigns, the yearly rent of 8s 2d. Furthermore, after the death of the said Roger Cowoop, the feofees and their heirs were to be seised of the property to the use of John Cowoop, son of the said Henry Cowoopp, and Agnes, his wife, for their lives (if Agnes outlived her husband and kept herself sole and unmarried). The said John Cowoopp and Agnes, were to yield all such rents, customs and services as were before recited. The remainder of the premises to the said Henry Cowoopp and his heirs for ever.

[Membrane 3d]

Rossindale

At the halmote of the manor of Accrington held there on Friday, 30th May, 9 Elizabeth I [1567] before the steward aforesaid, Edmund Tailior, then greave of Rossindale, surrendered one messuage, other buildings, lands, tenements, meadows, grazing lands, pastures and mosses in Gamblesyd and Wullfinden in the Forest of Rossindale, annual rent to the Queen 7s, in the tenure of John Ormerod of Gambleside, junior, and William Hanson, which the said John Ormerod had delivered to him, to Henry, son of the said John Ormerod, and his heirs, as feofees according to the intent. Admittance sought and granted. Fine 7s by the pledge of John Holt.

The intent was that Henry Ormerod and his heirs were to be seised of the property to the use of the said Henry for life, he paying to the said John Ormerod and his assigns yearly during the term at the feasts of Easter and St. Michael the Archangel [29th September] 10s by even portions, if John lived so long. If John died, then Henry was to pay to John's heirs the yearly rent of 7s. And further, if Isabel, Henry's wife, outlived him, then she should have and enjoy all such lands and tenements as were in the occupation of the above named William Hanson and two crofts lying above the house during her widowhood, she paying yearly to the Queen 7s and to the said John Ormerod and his heirs another 7s.

Henry, son and heir of Dionysius Hauworth, late of Constableleigh, deceased, complained against John, son of John Hauworth, late of Okenheadwood, deceased, in a plea of land, viz because the defendant had disseised the plaintiff of one messuage, other buildings, lands and tenements, meadows, grazing lands, pastures and mosses in Okenheadwood in the Forest of Rossindale, annual rent to the Queen 21s 8d, now or lately in the tenure of the said John Hauworth, the son, and Robert, his son. The plaintiff said the defendant had detained the premises from him for a long time and continued to do so. He also said that Dionysius Hauworth, his father, was the son and heir of Ottiwell Hauworth, now deceased, and that the said Ottiwell took *inter alia* the premises from the late king, Henry VII, by virtue of a commission at the time of the division of the said Forest, by which the same Ottiwell, the plaintiff, [*sic*] claimed title to the messuage, etc. The defendant denied the charge. A day was given the parties until the next halmote of the manor held at Accrington on Friday, 26th May, 12 Elizabeth [1570]. And meanwhile a jury of twenty-four good and lawful men, Queen's tenants of the New Hold, was chosen by the greaves of the New Hold to make judgement between the parties. The jury were John Robinson of Oldlaund, Christopher Hartley of Barrowford, John Hargreaves of the same, Nicholas Robinson, junior, Edmund Stephanson, Christopher Robinson, son of Lawrence, Roger Hartley of Wycolar, Christopher Hartley of the same, Hugh Pillinge, Christopher Bridge of Greaveclough, John Lord, son of James, Alexander Hauworth of Dedwenclough, William Yate, George Hauworth of Musbury, Oliver Ormerod of Wullfinden, Francis Bridge of Musbury, Robert Hauworth of Accrington, George Ryley, Robert Ryley and Richard Pemberton. To discuss and agree in court here concerning the giving of their verdict on the said matter, they retired behind the curtain.[?] Afterwards, having discussed the matter amongst themselves for a long time, being fully agreed and being prepared to give their verdict, came back to the bar. The said Henry Hauworth was solemnly summoned but did not come or proceed with his action. Therefore he was in mercy of the court and the said John Hauworth, son of John, was to go without a day in respect thereof.

[*In the margin*] Amercement 3d.

Sum of this court 40s ¼d.

Sum of these two halmotes aforesaid £7 12s 4¼d
In the charge of the greaves of :
Accrington Old Hold 16s 8d total of fines for land
Accrinton New Hold nothing
Rossendale 115s 8¼d; fines for land 112s 1d, amercements 3s 7d
Haslingden 20s; fines for land 17s, amercements 3s
Approved and charged in the 12th year of Queen Elizabeth.

Ightenhill
Halmote of the manor of Ightenhill held at Bruneley, Thursday, 22nd December, 12 Elizabeth I [1569] before John Towneley, esq., chief steward there.

Inquisition taken there for the Queen to make enquiry upon the oaths of Robert Roo, John Houghton, John Hargreaves of Goldshaie, Francis Webster, Robert

Houghton, Robert Whitacar of Healey, Michael[?] Aspeden, Robert Jackeson of Redley, Nicholas Hargreaves, John Higgyn, Henry Willysell, Richard Acroyd, Richard Ingham of Bruneleywood and Robert Towne.

John Hancocke died about the date of the last court seised of one close of land called Dubcarr, on the east side of Padiham, containing 5 acres, and now or lately in the tenure of Miles Londisdale and William Sonkie. And also of 1½d of rent in Sabdenbank. William Hancocke was his brother and next heir and of full age. Admittance sought and granted. Fine 21½d by the pledge of Hugh Hallstead.

John Marshall (2d), Henry Whitacar of Padiham (12d), John Watmough (12d), John Cronkshaie alias Tailior (12d) and Nicholas Saiger of Bruneley (12d) because they kept illegal games in their houses.

Anne Towneley (3s 4d), widow, lately wife of Nicholas Towneley of Roile, esq., deceased, because she made a rescue upon the greave of Ightenhill and hindered in the execution of his office.

Whereas a penalty of 20s was imposed at the last court that the aforesaid Anne Towneley, widow, should lay open one way used from ancient times through her land and tenement called Roilhill and because the said Anne had not laid open the way to the grave damage of her neighbours she was in mercy of the court. 20s.

One of the sons of John Robinson (12d) because he broke the Queen's fold in M'sden.

Amercements 29s 4d.

[Membrane 4]

John Leigh of Croston surrendered by John Kippax, a tenant of the Queen, two parts of one messuage and other buildings and two parts of 11 acres 1½ roods of land in Little Mersden called the lower part of Claver hole, now or lately in the tenure of Thomas Leigh and John Higgen and Jennet, his wife, or their assigns, to the said John Higgyn, Jennet, his wife, and their legitimately begotten children and their assigns from 15th April 1577 for fourteen years. Admittance sought and granted. An annual rent of 17s was payable to the said John Leigh and his heirs at the feasts of Pentecost and St. Martin the Bishop in Winter [11th November] by equal portions or within ten days following. Fine 2s by the pledge of John Kippax.

John Leigh of Croston surrendered by John Kippax, a tenant of the Queen, the third part of one messuage and other buildings and the third part of 11 acres 1½ roods of land in Little M'sden called the lower part of Claverhole, now in the tenure of Thomas Leigh and John Higgen and Jennet, his wife, or their assigns, to the said Thomas Leigh and his assigns from 15th April 1577 for fourteen years. Admittance sought and granted. An annual rent of 8s 10d was payable to John Leigh and his heirs at the feasts of Pentecost and St. Martin the Bishop in Winter [11th November] by equal portions or within ten days following. Fine 14d by the pledge of John Kippax.

John Hutchen of Wurstorne surrendered by Robert Ingham, a tenant of the Queen, half of one messuage and other buildings and half of 5 acres 1 rood of land in Haberghameves, to Nicholas Dobson of Sawreave and his heirs for ever as feofees according to the intent. Admittance sought and granted. Fine 11d by the pledge of John Tattersall.

The intent was that Nicholas Dobson and his heirs should be seised of the property (after the determination of certain uses thereof made as by the court rolls may appear) to the use of Christabel, wife of John Hutchen, for life.

Thomas Willysell of Scolebanck and Ingram, his son, surrendered by Richard Smythez, deputy of John Towneley, esq., chief steward, certain lands, tenements, meadows, grazing lands and pastures containing 6 acres lying in Scolebancke in the vill of Padiham, to Robert Willysell, brother of the said Thomas, and his heirs according to the intent. Admittance sought and granted. Fine 2s by the pledge of Bernard Towneley.

The intent was that Robert Willysell and his heirs should be seised of the property (in consideration of and recompense for all debts, duties and demands which the said Thomas Willysell owed to the said Robert Willysell either by reason of the last will and testament of James Willysell, their father, deceased, or by the administration of his goods or for any other cause or consideration) to the use of him, the said Robert Willysell and his assigns from the feast of the Purification of Our Blessed Lady the Virgin [2nd February] next for eleven years. And the same 6 acres were to be limited and appointed by Richard Grymeshaie, esq., and John Grymeshaie, his son, or one of them, of that part of land, parcel of the Scolebancke, which was in the tenure of the same Thomas Willysell and his assigns. Provided always that if the said Thomas Willysell or his assigns paid to the said Robert Willysell, his executors or assigns, twenty-five marks[1] at any of the feast days of the Purification of Our Blessed Lady which should be within the term of eleven years or so much thereof as should not then be come up, allowing and rebating 33s 4d yearly of the same sum, that then the said Robert Willysell and his heirs should be seised of the premises to such use and intent and to such person as the same premises ought to descend or come unto and that then this surrender above to be merely frustrate and the same Robert, immediately after such payment made, quietly to avoid the possession of the premises.

Sum of this halmote 37s 6½d.

Ightenhill
Halmote of the manor of Ightenhill held at Bruneley, Thursday, 18th May, 12 Elizabeth I [1570] before John Towneley, esq., chief steward there.

Inquisition taken there for the Queen to make enquiry upon the oaths of Edmund Starkie, gent., Hugh Shutleworth, gent., Henry Ryley, gent., Thomas Willysell, John

---

[1] A mark was a unit of accounting equalling 13s 4d.

44

Tattersall, John Woodrof, Robert Jackeson of Reidley, Nicholas Hargreaves of Edgend, Richard Tattersal, Richard Acroid, Robert Ingham, Richard Pollard, Francis Webster, Robert Brerecliff, Robert Roo and James Bancrofte.

John Pullane was elected constable of Bruneley; John Hutchen and Richard Leigh, constables of Haberghmeves; John Shefeld, constable of Padiham; Nicholas Russheton, John Woodrof and James Folldes, greaves of Bruneley.

James Leigh (12d) because he kept illegal games in his house.

Robert Towne (12d) because he frequently played at cards.

The late wife of William Raven (1d) because she dug turfs upon le Bruneley Mor contrary to the bye-laws and carried away two cartloads.

Lawrence Fletcher (2d) and Richard Bancrofte (2d) did likewise.

Whereas a penalty of 20s was imposed at the last court that Anne Towneley, widow, should lay open one way used since ancient times through her land and tenement called Roylhill. And she had not laid open the said way according to the order of the said jury to her neighbours' harm. Therefore she was in mercy. Amercements 22s 5d.

At the halmote of the manor of Ightenhill held at Bruneley, Thursday, 14th June, 8 Elizabeth I [1566] before the steward aforesaid, Henry Towneley, esq., Alexander, son of John Russheworth, esq., Robert, son and heir of William Barcrofte, gent., and William, son of Henry Barcrofte, gent., (at the request of Lawrence Habergham, gent.) surrendered one messuage and 65 acres of land in Habergham within the jurisdiction of this court, to Lawrence, son and heir of the said Henry Towneley, Edmund Sterkie, John Hancock, gent., and John, son and heir apparent of Henry Ryley, gent., and their heirs for ever as feofees according to indentures made by (1) the said Lawrence Habergham and (2) Nicholas Hancock of Lower Higham, gent., and dated 31st January 8 Elizabeth I [1565/6]. Admittance sought and granted. Fine 21s 8d by the pledge of the said Edmund Sterkye.

At the halmote of the manor of Ightenhill held at Bruneley, Thursday, 14th June, 8 Elizabeth I [1566] before the steward aforesaid, Lawrence Habergham, gent., surrendered one messuage called Oken Eves and 21½ acres of land in Habergh'm Eves within the jurisdiction of this court, to Lawrence, son and heir of Henry Towneley, esq., Edmund Sterkie, John Hancock, gent., and John, son and heir apparent of Henry Ryley, gent., and their heirs for ever as feofees according to an indenture made by (1) the said Lawrence Habergh'm and (2) Nicholas Hancock of Lower High'm, gent., dated 31st January 8 Elizabeth I [1565/6]. Admittance sought and granted. Fine 6s 10d by the pledge of John Hancock.

At the halmote of the manor of Ightenhill held at Bruneley, Tuesday, 25th May, 5 Elizabeth I [1563] before the steward aforesaid, Lawrence Haberiam, gent., surrendered one messuage, one croft and one garden called Ganowe in Brunley and

Ightenhill containing 1 rood of land, to William Barcrofte, junior, and Robert Barcrofte and their heirs as feofees according to the intent. Admittance sought and granted. Fine 1d by the pledge of Nicholas Whitticare.

The intent was that William and Robert Barcrofte and their heirs should be seised of the property to the use of William Hergreves of the Yateffeilde and his heirs for ever. Provided always that the yearly rent of 5s should be paid to the said Lawrence Haberiam, his heirs, executors and assigns, for the life of John Smythe late of Brunlay, son of John Smythe, late of Brunley, deceased, at the feasts of Pentecost and St. Martin the Bishop in Winter [11th November] by even portions or within eight days following. If the rent was not paid after either of the feast days, then the feofees were to be seised of the property to the use of the said Lawrence Haberiam, his heirs and assigns, for ever.

At the halmote of the manor of Ightenhill held at Brunley, Wednesday, 11th December, 9 Elizabeth I [1566] before the steward aforesaid, Nicholas Robert of Symonstone and Margery, his wife, surrendered one close or parcel of land lying in the west part of Padiham containing 3 acres of oxgang land called Olde Heye, to Nicholas Halsted of Padiham and his heirs for ever. Admittance sought and granted. Fine 12d by the pledge of John Tattersall.

John Aithaulgh, feofee, (at the request of Nicholas Banester of Altham) surrendered by Edmund Sterkie, gent., a tenant of the Queen, two messuages and other buildings and 33 acres of land in Padiham, to the said Nicholas Banester and his heirs for ever. Admittance sought and granted. Fine 11s by the pledge of Henry Barcrofte.

Thomas Willysell and Ingram, his son, surrendered by Robert Roo, a tenant of the Queen, one close of land called le Ryefeild lying in Scolebanck containing 3 acres of land, to Miles Clayton of Fernyfold and his assigns from the feast of St. Michael the Archangel [29th September] next for six years. Admittance sought and granted. Fine 12d by the pledge of John Houghton.

The intent was that if Thomas Willysell, his executors or assigns, paid to Miles Clayton £5 6s 8d at one whole and entire payment at any time before the feast of St. Michael the Archangel [29th September] next, that then this surrender to be void and the said Thomas and Ingram, immediately upon such payment made, to stand and be in their former estate.

John Towneley, esq., farmer of the Queen's water mill in Bruneley said that, because of a weakness in the building and construction of the mill sluice or ditch, a great part of the water which was accustomed to run down to the mill by the said sluice or ditch had run out of the same sluice or ditch and also out of the mill pond, because of which the mill was unable to grind any corn. And so the said farmer had lost the profit of the mill for a long time, to the disinheriting of the Queen and to the grave damage of the farmer, to the value, etc. And, because the Queen's tenants of the oxgangland of this manor were formerly accustomed to make and build the said ditch and sluice, the farmer asked that it be inquired for the Queen by an inquisition of this manor concerning the defaults and failures of the tenants in the said matters, so that the water may be channelled back into the ditch and sluice and into its old course to the mill, at the costs of the tenants. Upon which information the said jurors or inquirers were charged upon their oaths to inquire about the aforementioned things. They said just as follows in English words.

[*In English*]

First we find that the Queen's farmer of the said mill for the time being shall make and uphold one half rod (after eight yards to the rod) next adjoining to the 'uppermoste Clowe as it nowe standeth.'

Item we find that Edm'de Towneley, esq., and his heirs shall make and uphold one rod of the like measure next adjoining to the said half rod for one oxgang of land lying in Roile and Cronckeshaie.

Item we find that Will'me Hallstead of Banckehowse and his heirs shall make and uphold one other rod for one oxgang of land called Banckehowse.

Item we find that John Tattersall of Piccopp and his heirs shall make and uphold one other rod for one oxgang lying in Pyccopp.

Item we find that Evan Haydock, gent., and his heirs shall make and uphold one other rod for one oxgang of land called Grymehowse.

Item we find that the said Edmund Towneley and his heirs shall make and uphold one other rod for one oxgang of land lying in Clyfton.

Item we find that John Tailior, Henry Tailior and Peter Cloughe and their heirs shall make and uphold one other rod for one oxgang of land now in the tenure of Thomas Towneley, gent.

Item we find that the said Edmund Towneley, esq., and his heirs shall make and uphold one other rod for one other oxgang of land in Royle and Cronckeshaie.

Item we find that Robert Ingh'm and his heirs shall make and uphold one other rod for one oxgang of land called Fullage.

Item we find that the said John Tattersall and his heirs shall make and uphold one other rod for one other oxgang of land in Pyccopp.

Item we find that Richard Woodrof and his heirs shall make and uphold one other rod for lands adjoining to the 'fourthe' beneath the bridge at the west end of Bruneley.

Item we find that William Foldes of Dans'howse and his heirs shall make and uphold one other rod for certain lands called Danserhowse.

Item we find that the said Edmund Towneley, esq., and his heirs shall make and uphold one other rod for the other oxgang of land in Clyfton.

Item we find that William Barcrofte of Barcrofte and Richard Tattersall of the Ridge and their heirs shall make and uphold two other rods for two houses and lands thereunto belonging lying in Bruneley now in the occupation of George Smythe and John Willson.

[*Membrane 5d*]

Item we find that the said Edmund Towneley, esq., and his heirs shall make and uphold fourteen rods for the said two oxgangs of land in Clyfton.

Item we find that the said Edmund Towneley and his heirs shall make and uphold ten rods for the said two oxgangs of land in Royle and Cronkshaie.

Item we find that the said John Tattersall and his heirs shall make and uphold ten rods for the said two oxgangs of land in Pyccopp.

Item we find that the said Owyne [*sic*] Haydock and his heirs shall make and uphold three rods and one yard for the said lands called Grymehouse.

Item we find that the said William Foldes and his heirs shall make and uphold two rods for the said lands called Danserhowse.

Item we find that the said William Hallsted and his heirs shall make and uphold one other rod for the said lands called Banckhowse.

Item we find that the said Richard Woodrof and his heirs shall make and uphold one other rod for his lands at the west end of Bruneley.

Item we find that John Tailior, Henry Tailior and Peter Cloughe and their heirs shall make and uphold one other rod for the said lands now in the occupation of Thomas Towneley.

Item we find that Robert Ingham and his heirs shall make and uphold one other rod for the said lands in Fullage, 'wch rode adioneth to the backe clowe.'

Hugh Hallstead and Thomas Boith complained against Thomas Ryley of Hawkshey and John Robinson of Haberh'meves, his tenant, in a plea of trespass because the defendants impeded and stopped up a certain course of water flowing in a certain channel within Habergh'meves to the great harm of the plaintiffs and of which the plaintiffs suffered damage to the value of £10. The defendants denied this. The jury of Hugh Shuttleworth, gent., Robert Ingham of Fullage, John Kippax, William Hartley of Bradley, Thomas Whitwha' of Lowe House, William Smythe of Hill, Francis Webster, Lawrence Whitacar of Padhi'm, John Houghton, Robert Whitacar of Healey, John Tattersall of Piccopp and William Lund, senior, found that the defendants had turned the said water from its ancient course. And that it ought to run in its ancient course. Thus the defendants were in mercy. Amercement 3d.

Sum of this halmote 64s 3d.

Sum total of these two halmotes in the charge of the greave of Ightenhill, 101s 9½d. Fines for land 49s 9½d, approved and charged the 12th year of Elizabeth the Queen.

Amercements 52s, approved and charged the year aforesaid.

[*Membrane 6*]

Colne
Halmote of the manor of Colne held there, Saturday, 5th November, 11 Elizabeth I [1569] before John Towneley, esq., chief steward there.

Inquisition taken there of the Old Hold for the Queen to make enquiry upon the oaths of Edward Marsedene, James Foldes, John Foldes, Henry Shawe, John Dryver, John Blaykeye, senior, John Ellote, John Mankynholes, John Tailior, William Harteley, Robert Bawdewyne, Henry Harteley alias Byrdie, Lawrence Wylson, John Walton and Henry Walton.

Lawrence Rydihalghe and Henry Boothman were elected greaves of Colne and M'sedene; Geoffrey Shawe was elected constable of Colne; Alexander Parker was elected constable of the vill of Colne; [*The word 'vill' has been written over an erased word.*]; John Harteley was elected constable of Mersdene.

Henry Bawedwyne (2d) of Wyteheade because he trespassed with his sheep on the common pasture within the halmote and manor of Colne and Marsedene. ['and Marsedene' *crossed out.*]

John Chambers (6d) and John Suell (excused) because they made an affray on each other. [*This entry has been added.*]
Amercements 8d.

Henry Townley, gent., Thomas Emote and John Kepas, surviving feofees, (at the request of William Lyster, esq.) surrendered by John Hyggyne, a tenant of the Queen, one messuage or tenement with its buildings in Great Mersdene, now or lately in the tenure of James Foldes and James Wilsone. And one other messuage or tenement with its buildings in Great Mersdene, now or lately in the tenure of Richard Ayertone. And also one close called Shakilshaye in Great Mersdene, now or lately in the tenure of James Robynsone alias Bowse, in all 38 acres, to the said William Lyster, esq., and his heirs for ever. Admittance sought and granted. Fine 12s 8d by the pledge of Henry Barcrofte, gent.

Afterwards, the said William Lyster, esq., surrendered the messuage in the tenure of James Foldes, and the messuage in the tenure of Richard Ayertone and the close of land called Shakilshaye in the tenure of James Robynson, in all 35 acres 3 roods, to Henry Barcrofte, gent., and his heirs for ever. Admittance sought. The said James Foldes forbade fine as he had his messuage for life. The said Richard Ayertone and Elizabeth, his wife, forbade fine as they had their messuage for life. The said Henry Barcrofte allowed the forbids in open court and was then admitted. Fine 11s 8d by the pledge of Henry Townleye.

Afterwards, the said William Lyster, esq., surrendered by Richard Smythes, deputy steward, one messuage and other buildings, meadows, pastures and grazing lands in Great Mersedene, now or lately in the tenure of James Wilson, containing

2 acres 1 rood, to the said James Wilsone and his heirs for ever. Admittance sought and granted. Fine 9d by the pledge of John Kepas.

Afterwards, the said William Lyster, esq., surrendered by Richard Smythies, deputy steward, one house, one barn and 6 falls of land in Great Mersedene, now or lately in the tenure of James Foldes, to the said James Foldes and his heirs for ever. Admittance sought and granted. Fine ½d by the pledge of James Wilsone.

John Lee of Worstone surrendered by John Kepas, a tenant of the Queen, two parts of one messuage and other buildings and two parts of 5 acres in Great Mersedene called Sowthefeld, now or lately in the tenure of Thomas Lee, John Higgyne and Jennet Higgyne, his wife, to the said John and Jennet Hyggyne and their children and assigns for fourteen years from 15th April 1577. Admittance sought. John Wilsone forbade fine because of an agreement made with him by the said Thomas Lee. John and Jennet Higgyne found pledge John Kepas to answer the forbid and admittance was then granted. An annual rent of 8s was payable during the term to John Lee and his heirs at the feasts of Pentecost and St. Martin the Bishop in Winter [11th November] or within ten days of the said feasts. Fine 12d by the pledge aforesaid.

John Lee of Worston surrendered by John Kepas, a tenant of the Queen, the third part of one messuage and other buildings and the third part of 5 acres in Great Marsedene called Sowthefelde, now or lately in the tenure of Thomas Lee, John Hyggyne and Jennet, his wife, to the said Thomas Lee and his assigns for fourteen years from 15th April 1577. Admittance sought. John Wilson forbade fine because of an agreement made with him by the said Thomas Lee. Thomas Lee found pledge John Kepas to answer the forbid and admittance was then granted. An annual rent of 4s was payable during the term to John Lee and his heirs at the feasts of Pentecost and St. Martin the Bishop in Winter [11th November] or within ten days of the feasts. Fine 6d by the pledge aforesaid.

James Smythe of Halcote Edge surrendered by William Hansone, a tenant of the Queen, one messuage and other buildings and 19½ acres of land lying upon Halcote Edge, now or lately in the tenure of the said James Smythe, to Christopher, son of the said James Smythe, and his heirs for ever. Admittance sought. James Smythe forbade fine as he had the premises for himself and his assigns for life and for [blank] his wife so that she had sufficient dower in the premises during her life. The same was granted to them by the said Christopher Smyth. Admittance was then granted. Fine 6s 6d. [No pledge given.]

Trawden

John Dryver and Elizabeth Dryver, widow, his mother, of Wynewall, complained against Lawrence Shuttleworthe of the same in a plea of making a partition of certain land and tenements in Wynewall which the said John Dryver and Elizabeth, his mother, held in common and undivided with the said Lawrence according to the custom of the manor and which partition was to be made according to the custom of the manor. A day was given them until the next halmote of the manor held at Colne on Friday 7th April 12 Elizabeth I [1570]. And meanwhile a jury of twenty-four good and lawful men, Queen's tenants of the New Hold, was chosen by the greaves of the New Hold to make judgement between the parties. The jury were Henry Kirshaie, Henry Hauworth, Evan Assheworth, Christopher Bridge of Dedwenclough, Oliver Ormerod of Crawshaieboth, Gilbert Birtwisill, Lawrence Holden, Ellis Cunlyf, Robert Hauworth, Christopher Hargreaves, George Ryley, Thomas Duckworth, Henry Banester, gent., Christopher Robinson of Barroford, junior, Nicholas Stevenson, James Robinson, Barnerd Blakey, John Nutter of Rugheley, James Hartley of Blackoo, Thomas Emot, William Hanson, Richard Hartley of Wynewall, Edmund Stevenson, and John Lorde alias Bolton.

[Membrane 6d]

[In English] The jury within last mentioned do present and find that a lawful partition is already made of the lands and tenements contained in the action between John Dryver and Lawrence Shuttleworth. And further find that Elizabeth Dryver and the said Lawrence Shutleworth do hold their lands and tenements undivided for that that no partition as yet is made between them. Amercement 2d.

Forest of Trawden

Inquisition taken there of the Forest for the Queen to make enquiry upon the oaths of Lawrence Robert of Wynewall, senior, James Harteley, junior, Lawrence Shotilworth, John Dryver, Geoffrey Harteleye of Trawedene, Lawrence Harteleye, Richard Harteleye, Robert Harteleye, Richard Harteleye, Robert Harteleye, Geoffrey Shakilton, junior, Richard Shakilton, Henry Harteley, Roger Harteley of Wycoler, Barnard Hartly, James Emote and John Foldes.

James Harteley of Wynewale, senior, was elected greave of Trawedene.
Sum of this court 33s 11½d.

Colne

Halmote of the manor of Colne held there Friday, 7th April, 12 Elizabeth I [1570] before John Townley, esq., chief steward there.

[No jury given]

Henry Banister of Parke hill, gent., surrendered by Richard Smythies, deputy steward, one messuage, one other house and one garden in Colne, now or lately in the tenure of James Banyster, to Robert, son and heir apparent of the said Henry Banester, and his heirs for ever. Admittance sought. Thomas Banester forbade fine as he had the premises for himself and his assigns for life. Robert Banester found pledge John Taylior to answer the forbid and admittance was then granted. Fine 1d by the pledge aforesaid.

51

Afterwards, the said Robert Banester surrendered the property to John Blaykey, junior, and his heirs for ever. Admittance sought and Thomas Banester made the same forbid. John Blaykeye found pledge John Swene to answer the forbid and admittance was then granted. Fine 1d by the pledge aforesaid.

Release. At the halmote of the manor held on Tuesday, 26th April, 11 Elizabeth I [1569] before the steward aforesaid, Thomas Emote and James, his son, surrendered and released, remised and quit claimed one messuage, other buildings and 10½ acres of land in Emote Lone, now or lately in the tenure of Elizabeth Emote and Thomas Emote, to the said Elizabeth Emote for life and after her death to the said Thomas Emote and his lawfully begotten heirs and in default of such issue the remainder thereof to William, son of Henry Emote, deceased, and his heirs for ever. Elizabeth, Thomas and William Emote sought admittance and it was granted. [*No fine given*] Pledge Henry Banester, gent.

Trawden

John Dryver of Wynewall complained against Lawrence Shuttleworth of the same in a plea of making partition of certain lands and tenements in Wynewall which John held in common and undivided with Lawrence according to the custom of the said manor. Lawrence refused to allow the partition, but then said that he could not deny that he and the plaintiff held the property in common and undivided and that a partition ought to be made between them. The greave was ordered to return twelve good and lawful men so that the partition may be made. The jury of Geoffrey Hartley of Trawden, Lawrence Hartley, Robert Hartley, Richard Hartley, James Hartley, Roger Hartley, Henry Hartley, Bernard Hartley of Wycolor, Christopher Hartley, John Foldes, Roger Hartley of Wynewall and James Hartley of the same found that a partition of the lands and tenements ought to be made in the following way. [*In English*] The jurors aforesaid present and find that Lawrence Shuttleworth shall have his part of land lying all after the land of Richard Hartley from the over end unto the lower end. And also that the said Lawrence shall follow the 'more dole diche' at Tunstead where they did vary and did not agree. And also that the said Lawrence shall have the three acres of over measure lying at the lower side of his lands and that to be square and as broad at the one end as at the other end. Therefore it is considered that the said partition ought to be kept firm and stable for ever. Amercement 1d.

Lawrence Robert and James Hartley of Wynewall, junior, complained against James Hartley of the same, senior, in a plea of trespass. They said that the plaintiffs and defendants held certain lands and tenements in Wynewall in common and undivided and had to make and uphold their part and portion of the fences according to the amount of their rent there until a partition of the lands and tenements was made between them. The partition was to have been made by the agreement of the plaintiffs and the defendant within four years from 15th April last before the date of this court. The defendant said he did not have to make the fences as the plaintiffs alleged and was prepared to prove it. The parties placed themselves on the country. The jury of Geoffrey Shacleden of Trawden, junior, Roger Hartley of the same, Richard Hartley of the same, Henry Hartley of the same, John Folldes of Wycolar, Bernard Hartley of the same, Christopher Hartley, Henry Banester of Parkehill, gent., Christopher Hartley of Barroford, Barnard Blakey of Blakey, William Smyth of Rughley and Richard Bibbye of the same found that both the plaintiffs and the defendant ought to make and uphold sufficiently the fences on their lands and tenements according to the amount of their rents. Thus the defendant was in mercy. Amercement 2d.

Sum of this court 5d.

[Membrane 7]

Colne
Halmote of the manor of Colne held there on Saturday, 27th May, 12 Elizabeth I [1570] before John Townleye, esq., chief steward there.

Inquisition taken there for the Queen to make enquiry upon the oaths of John Hartley of Adm'gill, John Hargreaves of Golldshaie, Henry Shawe, William Hanson, John Dryver, John Foldes, John Ellot, John Tailior, William Hartley, Henry Wallton, Henry Hartley alias Byrdee, Robert Bawdwen, John Mankenholes, James Foldes and Christopher Hartley of Barrowford.

John Higgyn (2d) because he dug and got two cartloads of turfs upon the common pasture of Shelfeld. John Parker (2d), Henry Boithe (2d) and Henry Bawdwen (2d) did likewise.

Henry Manknoles (4d) because he trespassed upon the common pasture of Sholfeld with 40 sheep.

Henry Bawdwen (2d) of Wethead, Christopher Bawdwen (2d) of the same, senior, and Nicholas Bawdwen (2d) because they kept about 12 sheep upon the common pasture aforesaid.

Edward Hartley (4d) of Trawden because he trespassed upon the common pasture aforesaid with a horse.

Nicholas Robinson alias Thurnyholme (4d) because he over stocked [*crossed out*] trespassed upon the common pasture aforesaid with 20 sheep.

John Willson (2d) because he kept strangers' geese upon the common pasture aforesaid.

[*Total of amercements not given*]

William Lyster of Myddoppe, esq., surrendered by Christopher Harteley of Baroforthe, a tenant of the Queen, a parcel of land in Colne between le churche style and the house in which Lawrence Blaykeye lived, annual rent to the Queen 1d,

53

to Henry Banester of Parkehyll, gent., and his heirs for ever. Admittance sought and granted. Fine 1d by the pledge of John Taylior.

John Scale surrendered by Richard Smythies, deputy steward, a parcel of land in Colne in a close called Turnercrooke containing 1 rood of land, now or lately in the tenure of Henry Mytchell, to Nicholas Mytchell of Colne and his heirs for ever. Admittance sought and granted. Fine 1d by the pledge of Robert Harteley.

Gilbert Harteley of Great Mersdene surrendered certain buildings, a part of the buildings of Swynden, and 8 acres 23 falls[1] of land in Great Marsedene, now or lately in the tenure of the said Gilbert Harteleye, to Geoffrey Shawe of Colne and John Foldes of Carrie bridge and their heirs as feofees according to the intent. Admittance sought and granted. Fine 2s 8d by the pledge of Robert Harteleye.

The intent was that the feofees were to be seised of the property to the use of the said Gilbert Harteleye and Agnes, his wife, for their lives, and after their deaths to the uses given in Gilbert's will.

Henry Barcrofte of Lodge, gent., surrendered by James Foldes of Trawedene, a tenant of the Queen, one messuage, other buildings, lands, tenements, meadows, pastures and grazing lands in Great Mersedene containing 12 acres, now or lately in the tenure of James Foldes of Lee, to John Hyggyne of Little Mersedene and Robert Bawdewyne of Great Mersedene and their heirs as feofees according to the intent. Admittance sought and granted. Fine 8s by the pledge of James Foldes of Trawedene.

The intent was that the feofees were to be seised of the property to the use of James Foldes of the Lee and his assigns for life, paying yearly the rent of 29s to the said Henry Barcrofte and his heirs at the feasts of Pentecost and St. Martin the Bishop in Winter [11th November] and doing the services which James Foldes had been accustomed to do to William Lyster of Myddoppe, esq. After the death of James Foldes, the feofees were to be seised of half of the messuage and lands to the use of Ellen, wife of the said James, and her assigns for life, paying to the said Henry Barcrofte half of the rents and services. And to be seised of the other half to the use of Robert, son of the said James Foldes, and his assigns for life, paying to the said Henry Barcrofte the other half of the rents and services. If Ellen died before Robert, then the feofees were to be seised of her half to the use of the said Robert for life. If Robert died before his father, then Elizabeth, daughter of the said James, was to occupy and enjoy Robert's half after the death of her father until Henry Barcrofte had paid her, her heirs, executors or assigns, £4 10s. The remainder of the said messuage, etc. to the use of the said Henry Barcrofte and his heirs for ever.

At the halmote of the manor of Colne held there on Thursday, 9th December, 11 Elizabeth I [1568] before the said steward, it was presented that Henry Wallton of Barcarhowse died about the date of the last court seised of one messuage called le

---

[1] A fall of land was the same as a square rod, pole or perch.

Barcarhouse, other buildings and 36 acres of land in Great M'sden. John Wallton was his son and next heir and was of full age. Admittance sought and granted. Fine 12s by the pledge of John Robinson of Goldshaye.

[*Membrane 7d*]

John Ellote and William Harteley of Bradeleye (at the request of John Ellote, junior, son of the said John Ellote) surrendered one messuage, 13 acres of land, 1 rood of land of one penny rent in Alkyncotes within the vill of Colne, to the said John Ellote, junior, and his lawful heirs, and in default of such issue to the right heirs of the said John for ever. Admittance sought. John Ellote the father forbade fine as he had all the premises for life. John Ellote the son allowed the forbid in open court and was then admitted. Fine 4s 5½d by the pledge of Henry Shawe.

At the halmote of the manor of Colne held there on Thursday, 9th December, 11 Elizabeth I [1568] before the steward aforesaid, John Robynsone of Goldeshaybooth and Agnes, his wife, surrendered by Nicholas Michell of Colne, a tenant of the Queen, half of one messuage, half of two barns, half of one garden and 7½ acres of arable and meadowland in Colne or in the Forest of Trawedene, now or lately in the tenure of the said John Robynsone and John Huet, to Henry, second son of the said John Robynsone, Barnard, son and heir apparent of Barnard Parker of Alkincotes, John, son of Thomas Robynsone, and Barnard Harteley of Lawnde and their heirs as feofees according to an indenture dated 20th August 9 Elizabeth I [1567] and made by (1) the said John Robynson and (2) James Wilsone. Admittance sought and granted. Fine 2s 6d by the pledge of John Waltone.

At the halmote of the manor of Colne held there [*blank*] 9 Elizabeth I [1566/7] before the steward aforesaid, Thomas Lyster of Westebie, esq., and John Lyster, his brother, surrendered by Lawrence Hab'iam, gent., a tenant of the Queen, the third part of three messuages and other buildings and the third part of 48 acres 1 rood of land, being a part of Holte Howse in Alkincotes within the halmote of the manor aforesaid, to Henry Townley of Barnesyde, gent., and his heirs for ever. Admittance sought. Jennet, wife of James Bollarde, forbade fine for her dower. Henry Townley found pledge Henry Barcrofte to answer the forbid and was then admitted. Fine 5s 4d by the pledge aforesaid.

Robert Robynson complained against Henry Waltone, junior, in a plea of land saying that Henry had detained from him one parcel of land on the east side of one barn belonging to the plaintiff in Great Mersedene to the plaintiff's damage of 66s 8d. The defendant denied the charge. The jury of John Mankynholles, James Foldes, Nicholas Mychell of Colne, Nicholas Mychell of Olde Earthe, Geoffrey Shawe, John Swayne, Henry Hyggyne, Robert Harteley, Robert Bawdewyne, Gilbert Harteley, Edmund Ridihailghe and John Ellote found [*In English*] That Robert Robynsone has no lands on the east side of his barn, but that the said Robert Robynsone ought to have liberty in the lands of Henry Walton for the space of one week betwixt the feasts of Saint Michael the Archangel [29th September] and St.

Martin the Bishop in Winter [11th November] to repair the same barn. And if the same barn falls into decay by any chance, then the same Robert to have liberty to repair the same at all times when need shall require. Thus it was considered by the court that the plaintiff was in mercy for his unjust plea. Amercement 2d.

Forest of Trawden

Inquisition taken there for the Forest to make enquiry for the Queen upon the oaths of Roger Herteley of Wycolar, Barnard Herteley of the same, Christopher Herteley, junior, of the same, James Herteley of Wynewall, senior, Peter Herteley of the same, Richard Shakilton of Trawedene, James Herteley, senior, of the same, James Harteley, junior, of the same, Henry Harteley of the same, Roger Herteley of the same, Robert Herteley of the same, Richard Harteley of the same, Lawrence Herteleye of the same, Lawrence Robert of the same and James Herteley, junior, of Wynewall.

The jury presented that all was well within the Forest of Trawden.

Release in Colne

John Scale surrendered, and for himself and his heirs released, remised and quit claimed all right, title, estate, claim and demand which he had or in future may have had in all those lands, tenements, meadows, pastures and grazing lands in Colne, now or lately in the tenure of John Foldes, to the said John Folldes and his heirs for ever. Admittance sought and granted. Fine [*blank*]. [*No pledge given*]
Sum of this halmote 37s 5d

Sum total of these two halmotes 71s 9d approved and charged the 12th year of
Elizabeth the Queen
Colne 71s 4d. Fines for land, 68s 4d; amercements 3s.
Trawden 5d, total of amercements.
[*Membrane 8*]

Penhill
Halmote of the manor of Ightenhill held at Heigham, Tuesday, 25th October, 11 Elizabeth I [1569] before John Townley, esq., chief steward there.

Inquisition taken there for the Queen to make enquiry upon the oaths of Henry Banester, gent., Christopher Herteley, junior, of Baroforthe, John Hergreves of the same, Christopher Nutter, Richard Croke of Westclose, Edward Hargreves, Hugh Moore, John Hargreves of Goldeshaye, Nicholas Stevesone [*sic*], Robert Jacsone, Richard Nutter, James Robynsone of Bareley, Henry Robynsone, Thomas Varley, John Mankenholes, John Smythe of Roighe Heyhe and Nicholas Bawedewyne.

John Robynsone of Olde Lawnde was elected greave of Pendle.

Edmund Stevenson (8d) because he kept an illegal way in his land and tenement between Newchurche in Pendill and Tyndsted.

Amercements 8d.

Henry Townleye, gent., surrendered, by Thomas Rylaye, a tenant of the Queen, one water corn mill in the Forest of Pendle called le Carre mylne with all the watercourses to and from the said mill and all the soke and suit of the tenants of the New Hold within the Forest of Pendle belonging to the said mill in any way, annual rent to the Queen 20s, to Thomas, son and heir apparent of Thomas Lyster of Westbie, esq., Richard Smythes, Lawrence Townley, gent., and John Harteley of Admergill, yeoman, and their heirs as feofees according to indentures made by (1) the said Henry Townleye, (2) John Townley of Cornafelde, esq., and (3) Ellen Townley, widow, mother of the said Henry, dated 19th July 10 Elizabeth I [1568]. Admittance sought and granted. Fine 20s by the pledge of Thomas Rylaye.

Richard Nutter of Goldeshaye and Agnes, his wife, surrendered by Nicholas Moore, a tenant of the Queen, half of 1 acre of turbary in Goldeshay, annual rent to the Queen 1d, now or lately in the tenure of the said Richard Nutter, as it is marked out with metes and bounds in a certain place called 'litle mosse heade', to Hugh Moore of Heigham Deyne and his heirs for ever. Admittance sought and granted. Fine 1d by the pledge of Henry Banester.

John Harteley and Isabel, his wife, surrendered one messuage, other buildings, lands, tenements, meadows, pastures, grazing lands and mosses in le Fence, annual rent to the Queen 2s 6d, now or lately in the tenure of George Wylkynsone, to the said George Wilkynsone, and Jennet, his wife, and their assigns for the lives of the said John and Isabel Herteley. Admittance sought and granted. An annual rent of 2s 6d was payable to John and Isabel Herteley if lawfully asked for. Fine 2s 6d by the pledge of Hugh Moore.

At the halmote of the manor aforesaid held at Heigham, Tuesday, 10th December, 9 Elizabeth I [1566] before the steward aforesaid, Edmund Parker, a tenant of the Queen, surrendered one messuage, lands and tenements, meadows, pastures and grazing lands, now or lately in the tenure of Robert Robinsone and Roger Nowell of Fence, annual rent to the Queen 2s 8d, which the said Roger Nowell delivered to him, to James Dicconson for a term of years for which the said Roger Nowell had the property. Admittance sought and granted. Fine 2s 8d by the pledge of James Hergreves.

[In English] Memorandum that at the halmote of the manor of Ightenhill held at Higham the second day of December in the tenth year of our sovereign lady Queen Elizabeth [1567] by the inquisition there chosen to inquire for our said sovereign lady, there was a pain laid that John Robinson of the Old Lawnd should make a hedge between him and John Nutter according to an order made between them.

Sum of this court 25s 10½d

[Membrane 8d]

57

Penhull

Halmote of the manor of Ightenhill held at Heighame, Thursday, 13th April, 12 Elizabeth I [1570] before John Townley, esq., chief steward there.

[*No jury given.*]

Henry Robynsone of Roighe Leighe, senior, surrendered by Nicholas Robynson, senior, greave of Pendle, one messuage, other buildings, lands, tenements, meadows, grazing lands and pastures in Roigh Leighe, annual rent to the Queen 5s ½d ¼d, now or lately in the tenure of the said Henry Robynsone. And also one other messuage, other buildings, lands, tenements, meadows, grazing lands, pastures and mosses in Firbarne, annual rent to the Queen 8d, now or lately in the tenure of the said Henry Robynsone, to Miles, son and heir apparent of the said Henry, and his heirs for ever according to the intent. Admittance sought and granted. Fine 5s 8½d ¼d by the pledge of Nicholas Robynson.

The intent was that Miles Robynsone would allow Henry Robynson to occupy and enjoy the property in Roigh Leighe for life. Provided always that Elizabeth, daughter of Richard Hyndle of Dysnoppe, (whom the said Miles Robynson would marry by the grace of God) and her assigns should have the fourth part of both properties after the death of the said Miles for her jointure and dower for life. The remainder of all the premises to the said Miles and his heirs for ever.

Barnard Blaykey, gent., a tenant of the Queen, surrendered one messuage and other buildings built thereon, lands, tenements, meadows, grazing lands, pastures and mosses in Over Barrowfurthe in the Forest of Pendle, annual rent to the Queen 16s ½d, which Christopher Robynsone, junior, delivered to him, to James Harteley, son of Barnard Herteleye of Lawnde, and Simon Blaykey, son and heir of Barnard Blaykeye, and their heirs as feofees according to the intent. Admittance sought and granted. Fine 16s 1½d by the pledge of Nicholas Robynson.

The intent was that the feofees were to be seised of the property in Overbarowefurthe in the tenure of Christopher Robynson the elder, to the use of the said Christopher Robynsone the younger for life. And after his death to the use of the lawful issue begotten betwixt the said Christopher Robynsone and Elizabeth Syngleton and for lack of such issue then to the right heirs of the said Christopher for ever. Provided always that the feofees should be seised of the third part of the said houses, buildings, and certain parcels of land of the yearly rent of 5s 6d, a parcel of the yearly rent of 16s 1½d, to the use of the said Elizabeth Syngletone for life for her jointure and dower. The feofees were also to allow Elizabeth to receive all the issues, profits and advantages from the parcels of land for life.

[Membrane 9]

Agnes Hartley, widow, by her attorney, Henry Hartley, complained against Nicholas Whitacar and Ellen, his wife, Henry Blakey, Elizabeth, his wife, and

Lawrence Blakey because they detained from her the fourth part of the fourth part of one messuage, other buildings, meadows, grazing lands, pastures and mosses in Rougheleighe in the Forest of Pendle, annual rent to the Queen 22s 2½d, as her dower, of which said messuage and other premises her husband, Henry Hartley died seised in his demesne as in fee according to the custom of the manor. The defendants said that Agnes ought not to have her dower in the property because Henry Hartley, her husband, was not seised of it either on the day he married Agnes or ever after, so that Agnes could not have been dowered thereof, nor did he die seised thereof. A day was given them until the next halmote of the manor held at Higham on Thursday, 13th April, 12 Elizabeth I [1570]. And meanwhile a jury of twenty-four was chosen by the greaves of the New Hold. The jury consisting of Ralph Hauworth, Lawrence Tailior of Musbery, John Hargreaves, William Jenkinson, Hugh Pilling, Oliver Romesbothom, George Ormerod, Henry Hauworth, Richard Wallmissley, Edward Ryley, Edmund Pilling, Edward Ryley, James Hartley of Wynewall, senior, James Emot of Wycolor, Peter Hartley of the same, Barnard Hartley of the same, Geoffrey Hartley of Trawden, Richard Hartley of the same, John Parker, Christopher Robinson alias Christopher of Lawes, James Robinson of Bawley, Richard More, Ellis Nutter and Edmund Robinson found that the plaintiff ought to have her right dower in the fourth part of the fourth part of the said messuage, etc. and that she was entitled to a widow's dower therein according to the custom of the manor. Thus the defendants were in mercy. Amercement 2d.

Sum of this court 22s ¼d

Penhull
Halmote of the manor of Ightenhill held at Heigham, Monday, 29th May, 12 Elizabeth I [1570] before John Townleye, esq., chief steward there.

Inquisition taken there for the Queen to make enquiry upon the oaths of Christopher Nutter, George Cronkeshaye, Richard Moore, Ellis Nutter, James Crooke, Christopher Herteley, senior, Christopher Robynson, son of Lawrence, Nicholas Bawedewyne, John Smythe, Thomas Verlaye, John Mankynholles, Christopher Robynsone of Barleye, Richard Nutter, John Hergreaves, Christopher Robynsone, junior, and John Parker.

George Wilkinson of Fence (4d) because he felled trees within John Towneley, esq.'s land and tenement.

Nicholas Hancock because he stopped up and blocked one usual way between le Dipe Clough and the way leading between Ov' Higham and Lower Higham called Higham Yate [*No amercement given.*]

Edmund Stephenson received a surrender of certain lands, tenements, meadows,

grazing lands and pastures with half of one messuage in the Forest of Pendle, annual rent to the Queen 3s 4d, before the date of this halmote and did not present the same. [*No amercement given.*]
Amercements 4d.

Nicholas Robynsone of Roigh Leigh, junior, surrendered by Nicholas Robynson of Roigh Leigh, senior, greave of Pendle, certain parcels of land in le Lawnde Heade, annual rent to the Queen 6d, now or lately in the tenure of William Herteley of Roigh Leigh, to the said William for thirteen years from 15th April last before the date of this halmote. Admittance sought and granted. Fine 6d by the pledge of Nicholas Robynson, senior.

Nicholas Robynsone of Roigh Leigh, junior, surrendered by Nicholas Robynson of Roigh Leigh, senior, greave of Pendle, certain parcels of land in le Lawnde Heade, annual rent to the Queen 6d, now or lately in the tenure of John Whiteheade of Roigh Leigh, to the said John for thirteen years from 15th April last before the date of this halmote. Admittance sought and granted. Fine 6d by the pledge of Nicholas Robynson, senior.

John Herteley of Fence surrendered by Nicholas Robynson of Roigh Leigh, senior, greave of Pendle, one messuage and other buildings, lands, tenements, meadows, grazing lands, pastures and mosses in le Fence, annual rent to the Queen 5s, now or lately in the tenure of Robert Asteley, bastard son of Robert Asteleye of Cragges, to the said Robert Asteleye, bastard, and his assigns for the life of the said John Herteley. Admittance sought. Jennet Emote forbade fine as much for herself for her dower as for Jane Emote by right of her inheritance. Robert Asteley found pledge James Hergreaves to answer the forbid and admittance was then granted. Fine 5s by the pledge of Nicholas Robynson, senior.

John Harteleye, Thomas Verlaye, Richard Verlay and James Robynsone surrendered (at the request of Elizabeth Verlaye, widow, and William, son of Thomas Verlaye,) one messuage and other buildings, lands, tenements, meadows, grazing lands and pastures in Bawlaye Boothe in the Forest of Pendle, annual rent to the Queen 15s, to the said William Verlaye and his heirs for ever. Admittance sought. The said Elizabeth Verlaye forbade fine as she had all the property for her life. Ellis Browne forbade fine for a certain parcel of the property, annual rent to the Queen 6s 8d, for a term of years not yet ended. William Verlay found pledge Nicholas Robynsone, senior, to answer Ellis Browne's forbid and granted in open court that the said Elizabeth Verlay should have the premises for life. Admittance was then granted. Fine 15s by the pledge of Nicholas Robynson.

[*Membrane 9d*]

Edmund Stevesone [*sic*] surrendered one house and a certain parcel of land and turbary in Black Leache, annual rent to the Queen 6d, now or lately in the tenure of Richard Hargraves of Goldeshaye, to the said Richard Hergreves and his assigns from 1st May last before the date of this halmote for thirty years. Admittance sought and granted. An annual rent of 6s 2d was payable to Edmund Stevesone and his heirs. Fine 6d by the pledge of John Nutter.

Edmund Robynsone, John Wodroffe, junior, and Robert Bulcocke, senior, surrendered by Richard Smythies, deputy steward, (at the request of Nicholas Robynsone, senior, James, his son, and Margaret, his wife,) the fourth part of one messuage and the fourth part of other buildings, lands, tenements, meadows, grazing lands and pastures in Roigh Leighe, annual rent to the Queen 4s 10¼d, now or lately in the tenure of the said Nicholas Robynsone, to John Robynsone of Goldeshaye and Christopher Bulcocke as feofees according to the intent. Admittance sought and granted. Fine 4s 10¼d by the pledge of Geoffrey Hargreves.

The intent was that the feofees were to be seised of the property to the use of Ellen Bulcocke of Whythalghe, widow, and her assigns for life for her jointure and dower. After her death, the feofees were to be seised to the same uses that Edmund Robynsone, John Wodroffe and Robert Bulcocke were seised as specified in a surrender made to them dated 23rd May 7 Elizabeth I [1565].

Nicholas Robynsone, senior, greave of Pendle, surrendered one messuage and other buildings, lands, tenements, meadows, grazing lands and pastures in le Fence, annual rent to the Queen 5s, now or lately in the tenure of John Harteleye, which the said John Harteley and Isabel, his wife, delivered to him, to Lawrence Peresone according to the intent. Admittance sought and granted. Fine 5s by the pledge of Nicholas Robynsone.

The intent was that Lawrence Peresone and his heirs were to be seised of the property to the use of himself and his assigns during the lives of the said John and Isabel. In consideration that the said Lawrence and his assigns should find and maintain the said John sufficiently with meat, drink and clothes for life, if the said John Herteley would be contented therewith. If not, then Lawrence was to pay to John 30s at the feasts of Pentecost and St. Martin the Bishop in Winter [11th November] yearly for life. If the sum of 30s was behind or unpaid in part or in all at either of the feasts, then Lawrence was to be seised to the use of the said John Herteley and his assigns during the life of the said John.

John Nutter and Robert Herteley (at the request of Robert Nutter and Christopher, his son and heir apparent,) surrendered certain lands and tenements, grazing lands, pastures and mosses in Newe Lawnde within the Forest of Pendle, annual rent to the Queen 11s 1¼d, now or lately in the tenure of the said Robert Nutter, to John, son of the said John Nutter, and Barnard Herteley of Lawnde and their heirs as feofees according to the intent. Admittance sought and granted. Fine 11s 1¼d by the pledge of [blank].

The intent was that the feofees were to be seised of the property to the use of the said Robert Nutter for life and after his death to the use of Christopher Nutter, his son and heir apparent, and his lawfully begotten heirs. In default of such issue, then the feofees were to be seised to the use of James Nutter, Christopher's brother, and his lawfully begotten heirs, and in default of such issue, to the right heirs of the said Robert for ever. Christopher was to pay to Robert's wife (if Robert happened to marry) £3 6s 8d yearly for life at the feasts of Easter and St. Michael the Archangel [29th September] or within ten days after each feast. If the sum of money was not paid, then the said John Nutter and Barnard Herteley were to be seised of the property to the use of Robert Nutter's wife for life for her jointure and dower. The remainder thereof was to be according to the remainders above written.

Sum of this court 42s 9½d.

Sum of the three halmotes within the greaveship of Pendle
£4 10s 8¼d
Fines for land, £4 9s 6¼d; amercements, 14d.
Charged and approved in the 12th year of Queen Elizabeth.

[Membrane 10]

Tottington
Halmote of the manor of Tottyngton held at Halcome, Thursday, 3rd November, 11 Elizabeth I [1569] before John Townleye, chief steward there.

Edward, Earl of Derbie, judge of Burie; Edmund Asheton, esq., judge of Chatt'ton, appeared in court.
The constables of Burie, Myddilton, Alcryngetone, and Chatterton and Foxedenton appeared in court.

Inquisition taken there for the Queen to make enquiry upon the oaths of Lawrence Rawstorne, gent., Richard Rawestorne, Charles Nuttowe, Richard Romsbothom, John Holte, Thomas Woode, Richard Boothe, Thomas Grenehalghe, James Asheworthe, John Coweoppe, Henry Coweoppe, Richard Rothewell, Ralph Haworthe, William Brooke and Thomas Rothwell.

Charles Holte, esq., was elected greave of Tottingtone; Thomas Grenehaulgh and Charles Nuttowe were elected constables; Richard Rawestorne and John Holte were elected affeerors; Lawrence Rawestorne and William Brooke were elected appraisers; Ralph Holden, esq., John Holte and James Asheworthe were elected pounders; Thomas Woode and John Coweoppe were elected moss lookers; Thomas Grenehalghe and Henry Coweoppe were elected fence lookers and Richard Romsbothome and Thurstan Hamere were elected aletasters.

Ralph Nuttall (4d) and Arthur Assheworth (4d) of Cowoop because they kept their fences open between their lands and tenements and the common pasture of

Tottington and because they trespassed on the said common pasture with their livestock.

Christopher Boith (4d) because he blocked up one usual way in his land and tenement in le Boithe.
Amercements 12d.

John Holte of Hollyngreave surrendered by Henry Burie, greave of Tottingtone, one messuage and 8 acres of land in Woode Heye with common of pasture and appurtenances in Tottingtone and part of land in Aldene, now or lately in the tenure of [blank], to Francis Shepilbothome and his heirs as feofees according to an indenture made by (1) the said John Holte and (2) Francis, son of Henry Shepilbothome of Shetelworthe, dated 4th August 11 Elizabeth I [1569]. Admittance sought. Isabel Holte forbade fine by Richard Holte for a certain term of years. Francis Shepilbothome found pledge Thomas Nabbes, junior, to answer the forbid and admittance was then granted. Fine 2s 8d by the pledge aforesaid.

Richard Rawstorne of Tottingtone complained against Richard, son of Christopher Holte, lately deceased, in a plea of trespass. The plaintiff said the defendant had taken possession of a close of land called Dyveleche and occupied the same from the feast of St. John the Baptist [24th June] last before the date of this halmote and that the plaintiff had suffered damage to the value of 20s. The defendant denied this. The jury of Thomas Woode, Charles Nuttowe, Richard Boothe, Thomas Grenehaulghe, William Brooke, Richard Romsbothom, Richard Rothewell, James Ashworth, John Coweoppe, Henry Coweoppe, senior, Thurstan Hamer and Thomas Nabbes, junior, found that the defendant did not occupy the land illegally but of his proper right. Therefore the plaintiff was in mercy for his false plea. Amercement 3d.

Fee of Tottington
Inquisition taken there for the Queen to make enquiry upon the oaths of William Overall, James Shippilbothom, Henry Shippilbothom, George Warberton, Thomas Lyvesaye, Robert Lyvesaye, Edmund Haywoode, John Woode, Roger Taylor, Thomas Ratclyffe, Robert Ashetone, Richard Romsbothome, Henry Stocke and John Harteleye.

Robert Hauworth (20d) and Lawrence Fletcher (20d) because they made an affray together.

Richard Holt (3s 4d) because he made an affray on Ellis Fletcher and drew blood on him.
Amercements 6s 8d

Sum of this halmote 10s 7d

Tottington
Halmote of the manor of Tottingtone held at Hoolcome, Tuesday, 6th June, 12 Elizabeth I [1570] before John Townleye, esq., chief steward there.

Inquisition taken there for the Queen to make enquiry upon the oaths of Lawrence Rawstorne, gent., Richard Rawestorne, Richard Romsbothome, Henry Coweoppe, John Coweoppe, Thurstan Hamer, Charles Nuttowe, John Holte, Thomas Grenehalghe, Thomas Woode, Ralph Bridge, Ralph Haworthe, James Asheworthe and Richard Boothe.

Thomas Knole (3s 4d) because he made an affray upon Nicholas Wheywall and drew blood.

Richard Bridge of Tottington (12d) because he made an affray upon Christopher Kay.

George Nuttall of Tottington (12d) because he made an affray upon Edmund Synddill.

Robert Heigh (8d) because he kept his fences open between his land and tenement and the land and tenement of Richard Rawstorne.
Amercements 6s.

[Membrane 10d]

Thomas Nabbes, senior, (12d) because he dug and broke the Queen's soil of the common pasture of Tottington and he had recently put a dike in that way to the harm of his neighbours who held the common pasture of the Queen of her aforesaid manor, to his profit where they are not able.[*sic*]

The relict of Oliver Lawe (12d), Richard Batersbie (6d), Edward Waler (8d), Charles Ridgate (6d), Hugh Birtwisyll, chaplain, (12d), John Heighe (6d), Oliver Taylior (6d), Geoffrey Lumas (16d), Thomas Bridge, senior, (12) and Peter Holte (12d) for doing likewise.
Amercements 9s.

Henry Holte, greave of Tottingtone, surrendered two messuages, six oxgangs of land, three parts of one oxgang of land, 72 acres of land called 'Rodlande' in the vill of Tottington with common of pasture and appurtenances in Tottington and part of land in Alledene. And also one other messuage with 25 acres of land in the vill of Etenffeilde called Chatteron Heyes with common of pasture and appurtenances in Tottington and part of land in Alden, which Thomas Nuttall of Tottington delivered to him, to Thomas, son of Ralph Nuttal, and his heirs for ever. Admittance sought. The said Thomas Nuttall forbade fine by his son Richard Nuttall as he had all the premises for life. The same was granted to him in open court by the said Thomas Nuttall, junior, who was then admitted. Fine 32s 4d by the pledge of Thomas Grenehaulghe.

Henry Holte, greave of Tottington, surrendered one barn and certain closes of land containing 8 acres 3 roods in Hole Howse with common of pasture and appurtenances in Tottington and part of land in Alldene, which George Nuttall and Francis Nuttall delivered to him, to John, son of Edmund Haworthe, and his heirs for ever. Admittance sought. Edmund Entwissill forbade fine for two parts of a certain parcel of land upon which a barn was built. John Haworthe found pledge Edmund Lawe to answer the forbid and was then admitted. Fine 2s 11d by the pledge aforesaid.

Henry Holte, greave of Tottingtone, surrendered one messuage and certain closes of land containing 18 acres called Lumcare with common of pasture and appurtenances in Tottingtone and part of land in Alldene, which Richard Nuttall of Nuttall and Charles, his son and heir apparent, delivered to him, to Richard, son of Ralph Nuttall, and his assigns from the feast of the Annunciation of the Blessed Virgin Mary [25th March] last before the date of this halmote for thirty-three years. Admittance sought and granted. Fine 6s by the pledge of Thomas Nabbes, senior, and Thomas Nabbes, junior. An annual rent of 20s 8d was payable to Richard and Charles Nuttowe and their heirs and assigns.

Christopher Boothe surrendered by Henry Holte, greave of Tottingtone, three closes of arable land, meadow and pasture containing 4½ acres, of which one close is called Firwoodlee, another Litlecrofte and the third Boothe Lawe and le Hilles, with common of pasture and appurtenances in Tottingtone, to Ralph Birrie and his assigns for five years from the feast of the Annunciation of the Blessed Virgin Mary [25th March] last before the date of this halmote. Admittance sought and granted. Fine 18d by the pledge of John Grenehaulghe.

Agnes Etenfelde complained against Richard Nuttowe, gent., (2d) in two pleas of debt to the value of 56s. The defendant denied this. The jury of Edmund Lawe, Robert Chadwicke, Christopher Nuttowe, Richard Romsbothome, Henry Burie, John Keye, Robert Werberton, Richard Rothewell, Ralph Pillyngtone[sic], Thomas Barlawe, Alexander Entewissill, and Peter Lomas found that the defendant ought to pay 40s of the debt to the plaintiff.

James Buckeley (2d) complained against Ralph Buckeleye in a plea of debt for 38s 4d. The defendant denied this and the jury found nothing so that the plaintiff was in mercy.

William Marcrofte complained against George Onsworthe (2d) in a plea of debt for 10s. The jury found 5s 10d so the defendant was in mercy.
Amercements 6d.

Fee of Tottington

Inquisition taken there for the Queen to make enquiry upon the oaths of Francis Grenehalghe, Henry Nuttall, Thomas Battersbie, Robert Rothwell, Thomas Barlawe, Richard Chatertone, Richard Hodgedene, John Harteleye, Edward Whittiker and John Cowper.

John Whitacar (4d) because he did not do suit.

Edward Holt of Ewood (3s 4d) because he made an affray on Alexander Holt.
Amercements 3s 8d.

Sum of this halmote 52s 11d.

Sum of the two halmotes of Todington aforesaid 63s 6d
Greave; 53s 2d; fines for land 45s 5d; amercements 7s 9d
Bailiff; 10s 4d total of amercements
Approved and charged in the 12th year of Queen Elizabeth.

COURT ROLL OF THE HONOR OF CLITHEROE MICHAELMAS 1570 - EASTER 1571

[Membrane 1]

Halmote of the manors of Chatburne, Worston and Penhulton held at Clitherowe Castle, Monday, 29th January 13 Elizabeth I [1570/1] before John Towneley, esq., chief steward there.

Inquisition taken there for the Queen to make enquiry upon the oaths of Thomas Robinson, Richard Kendall, senior, Thomas Talior, Edmund Dawson, John Dugdale, senior, Richard Kendall, junior, John Dugdale, junior, Christopher Migecocke, Richard Dugdale, John Dawson, Richard Hole, John Moore, Richard Mersden and Ottiwell Feilden.

Chatburne

Robert Banester was elected greave of Chatburne; John Harryson and Richard Woode were elected constables.

Richard Mylles (2d) because he cut down and felled certain trees called 'le hollens' in le Cowpasture of Chatburne.

Richard Dugdale (2d), James Harropp (2d), William Talior (2d), Thomas Chatburne (2d), Thomas Ryley (2d), John Harropp (2d) and Jennet Spenser (2d) did likewise.

Richard Mylles (2d) for not doing suit.
Amercements 18d.

Wurston

James Browne was elected greave of Wurston; Thomas Bretherton was elected constable.

William Hurste (2d) for not doing suit.
Amercements 2d.

Penhulton

Richard Mersden was elected greave of Pe'hulton; John Braddill, esq., and Richard M'sden were elected constables.

Francis Webster (6d) because kept open one gate called in English 'a fleke' in le pasture there.

Amercements 6d.

Chatburne

Richard Banester died about the last court seised of one messuage and 6 acres of rodeland in Chatburne. Robert Banester was his son and next heir and of full age. Admittance sought. Margaret Bolde, widow, forbade fine as she had the premises for life. John Bolde forbade fine because of a certain agreement thereof made to him after the death of the said Margaret. Robert Banester found pledge Richard Kendale, senior, to answer the forbids and was then admitted. Fine 2s by the pledge aforesaid.

Chatburne

Thomas Robynson surrendered by Christopher Corbrige, greave of Chatburne, one messuage, other buildings and 17 acres of oxgang land and one other acre of rodeland in Chatburne, to Christopher, son of Roger Nowell of Mearley, gent., Robert Taillyor, son of Thomas Tallyor, Christopher, son of Richard Kendale, and John Talyor, junior, son of John Taylior, senior, as feofees according to the intent. Admittance sought and granted. Fine 12s by the pledge of Richard Kendale, senior.

The intent was that the feofees were to be seised to the use of the said Thomas Robinson and his lawfully begotten heirs. And in default of such issue, then to the use of Richard Robinson, brother of the said Thomas, and his lawfully begotten heirs. And in default of such issue to the use of the right heirs of the said Thomas for ever.

James Browne, greave of Wyrston, surrendered 1 rood and 8 falls of land in Wurston in a certain place called Moorebuttes on the west side of the outer fence there, which Richard Grenacars delivered to him, to Christopher Migecocke and his heirs for ever. Admittance sought and granted. Fine 1d [?] by the pledge of Thomas Robynson.

Sum of this halmote 16s 3d.

Chatburne

Halmote of the manors of Chatburne, Wurston and Penhullton held at Clitherowe Castle, Monday, 11th June, 13 Elizabeth I [1571] before John Towneley, esq., chief steward there.

Inquisition taken there for the Queen to make enquiry upon the oaths of Thomas Robinson, Thomas Tailyor, Edmund Dawson, John Talyor, senior, William Smythes, Richard Kendale, senior, Robert Tailyor, Christopher Migecock, Richard

Kendale, junior, John Dawson of Wurston, William Harste, John More, John Woulton and Ottiwell Feilden.

Thomas Hodgson (2d), [*blank*] Deinys [*no amercement*], Adam Smythe (2d), Richard Mylles (2d), William Harryson (2d) and James Harroppp (2d) for not doing suit.

The wife of John Harroppe, deceased, (2d) because she overstocked le Cowe pasture with one cow.

The constable of Chatburne (8d) because he did not perform his office according to the order he put before the court and especially about shooting arrows.

Alice, lately wife of William Atkinson, (4d), because she overstocked the common fields of Chatburne with her livestock.

Thomas Ryley (2d), John Johnson (4d) and Thomas Nowell (4d) because they did not repair and maintain their part of the Queen's mill sufficiently.

John Goodshay (12d) because he got turfs in a certain moss place belonging to Alexander Houghton, gent.

Francis Webster (4d) because he kept his fences open to the damage of Ottiwell Feilden and his other neighbours.

James Altham surrendered by John Woulton, a tenant of the Queen, one toft and site of one house in Penhulton on the north side of Penhulton aforesaid adjoining one house and garden belonging to Ottiwell Feilden on the west side and bordering one garden and croft of John Woulton on the east and north side, containing 1 rood of land, now or lately in the tenure of the said James Altham, to Thomas Hammond, his heirs and assigns, for ever. Thomas Hammond sought admittance by Alexander Houghton, gent., and it was granted. Fine ½d by the pledge of John Woulton.

[*Membrane 1d*]

Penhulton

James Altham surrendered by John Woulton, a tenant of the Queen, the fourth part of one oxgang of oxgang land with all houses, buildings, gardens, orchards and other commodities belonging in Penhulton, to James, son of John Aspinall, and Ralph, son of John Farrand, as feofees according to the intent. Admittance sought and granted. Fine 16d and no more because of poverty by the pledge of John Woulton.

The intent was that the feofees were to be seised of the fourth part of the one oxgang of land to the use of the said James Altham for life. After his death, they were to be seised of the 'olde fyer howse' now standing upon part of the premises with a little garden adjoining and of 'twoe beddes' in a garden on the south side of the croft gate, to the use of Alison and Lettice Carryer, daughters of the late Robert Carryer, deceased, for their lives. And they were to be seised of the residue of the property to the use of Sir John Altham, priest, brother to the said James, for life. The remainder of all the premises was to the use of William Carryer, son of the said late Robert Carryer, and his heirs for ever.

Sum of this halmote 5s 8½d.

Sum of the said two halmotes 21s 11½d charged and approved in the 13th year of Queen Elizabeth.
Chatborne 18s 7d; fines for land 14s 1d; amercements 4s 6d.
Worston 2d total of amercements.
Penhulton 3s 2½d; fines for land 16½d; amercements 22d.

Penhull
Halmote of the manor of Ightenhill held at Higham, Tuesday, 23rd January, 13 Elizabeth I [1570/1] before John Towneley, esq., chief steward there.

Inquisition taken there for the Queen to make enquiry upon the oaths of John Parker, George Cronckeshaye, Richard More, John Hargreaves of Barrowford, Christopher Robinson, son of Lawrence, John Hargreaves of Sabden, John Robinson of Goldshey, John Hartley of Bareley, James Robinson, Richard Hartley of Whitelyeheyboith, Richard Nutter of Rougheley, Christopher Bawdwyne, son of Henry, James Croke of Oldland, Nicholas Robinson alias Roughe Nycoll and Edmund Stephenson.

John Nutter was elected greave of Pendle.
George Wilkinson (12d) because he obstructed Lawrence Pearson in the highway.
Lawrence Pearson (12d) because he made an affray on George Wilkinson.
Amercements 2s.

John Hargreaves of Lowerbarrowforth, senior, surrendered by Christopher Smythe, a tenant of the Queen, one messuage, other buildings and certain lands, tenements, meadows, grazing lands, pastures and mosses called Water Metinges, annual rent to the Queen 2s, in Lowerbarrowford in the Forest of Pendle, and now or lately in the tenure of John Walton and John Rob't, to Lawrence, one of the younger sons of the said John Hargreaves, for life after the death of the said John. Admittance sought and granted. Fine 2s by the pledge of John Robinson. It was agreed between the said John and Lawrence that Lawrence ought to pay 5s annually to John at the usual feasts in equal portions.
Edward Hargreaves surrendered by James Hargreaves, a tenant of the Queen, one messuage, other buildings, lands, tenements, meadows, grazing lands and pastures in Higham Deane in the Forest of Pendle, annual rent to the Queen 6s 8d,

now or lately in the tenure of John Hargreaves, to the said John and his heirs and assigns for ever. Admittance sought and granted. Fine 6s 8d by the pledge of Hugh Hargreaves.

Nicholas Robinson alias Roughe Nicoll surrendered by John Towneley, esq., chief steward there, five closes or parcels of land called Greystones in Rougheleigh in the Forest of Pendle, annual rent to the Queen 5s 6d, now or lately in the tenure of the said Nicholas Robinson, William Harteley and John Whitehead or their assigns, to Lawrence Towneley of Blackoo, gent., John Robinson of Old Lande, John Robinson of Sabden and Barnard Harteley of Lawnde, and their heirs as feofees according to an indenture made by (1) the said Nicholas Robinson and (2) a certain Henry Harteley dated 18th August 12 Elizabeth I [1570]. Admittance sought and granted. Fine 5s 6d by the pledge of Nicholas Robinson, senior.

Sum of the said recited halmote 16s 2d.

[*Membrane 2*]

Halmote of the manor of Ightenhill held at Higham, Tuesday, 12th June, 13 Elizabeth I [1571] before John Towneley, esq., chief steward there.

Inquisition taken there for the Queen to make enquiry upon the oaths of Thomas Ryley, Robert Jackeson, Christopher Hartley, son of Humphrey, Christopher Robinson, son of Christopher, Nicholas Bawdwen, John Smythe of Rougheleighe, John Mytton of the same, Thomas Verley, James Robinson of Bareley, John Mankenhoyles, Richard Nutter of Goldshay, John Hargreaves of the same, Richard More, Hugh More and John Parker.

James Mytton of Lowerbarrowforde (12d) because he did not make his boundary walls.[*?*]

James Parker, son of Miles, (12d) because he made an affray on the relict of the late James Ballerde.

The said James (12d) and Thomas Ryley (12d) of Chatburne because they made an affray together and drew blood.

Edmund Stephaneson (6d[*crossed out*]12d) because he had an unlawful way within his land and tenement between le Newechurche in Pendle and le Tyndehead Yate.

Edmund Robynson, son of John Robinson of Oldlawnde, Ellis Robinson, and James, son of Nicholas Robinson, (at the request of John Hargreaves of Goldshaie and James, his son and heir apparent,) surrendered by Leonard Cronckeshay, a tenant of the Queen, half of one messuage, other buildings, lands, tenements, meadows, grazing lands, and pastures in le Fence within a parcel of Goldshayboith in the Forest of Pendle, annual rent to the Queen 2s 4d, now or lately in the tenure of John Tittrington and Roger Nowell, to Robert, son of Henry Shawe of Colne, Thomas, son and heir apparent of John Robinson of Sabden, John, son and heir apparent of Leonard Cronckeshaie of Westeclose, and Thomas, son and heir apparent of Robert Whitacar, and their heirs as feofees according to indentures made by (1) the said John Hargreaves and (2) Thomas Whitacar of Holme, gent., and Robert Whitacar, his son and heir apparent, dated 30th September 12 Elizabeth I [1570]. Admittance sought and granted. Fine 2s 4d by the pledge of Henry Hartley.

James Robinson and Christopher Robinson (at the request of Christopher Bulkocke) surrendered one messuage and other buildings, meadows, grazing lands and pastures in Whyteleyhayboith in the Forest of Pendle, annual rent to the Queen 25s 10d, now or lately in the tenure of the said Christopher Bulkocke and Nicholas Robinson, to the said Christopher Bulkocke, his heirs and assigns for ever. Admittance sought. Nicholas Robinson forbade fine by the right of Ellen, his wife, as she had a fourth part of the premises for life. The same was granted to her in open court by Christopher Bulkocke and he was then admitted. Fine 25s 10d by the pledge of Edmund Robinson.

James, son and heir of Nicholas Robinson, surrendered one house and certain parcels of land, meadow, grazing land and pasture in Rougheley in the Forest of Pendle, annual rent to the Queen 18d, now or lately in the tenure of William Tyndale, to the said William and his assigns for a term of years specified in a surrender made to him by the said Nicholas Robinson in the sixth year of the Queen's reign [1563/4]. Admittance sought and granted. Fine 18d by the pledge of James Robinson.

Lawrence Stevenson surrendered by John Robinson of Goldshaie, a tenant of the Queen, one messuage, other buildings, lands, meadows, grazing lands and pastures in Goldshaiebothe in the Forest of Pendle, annual rent to the Queen 11s, now or lately in the tenure of the said Lawrence and his assigns, to Edmund Stevenson, his son, and his heirs for ever. Admittance sought. Christopher Harteley forbade fine by the right of the said Lawrence and Alice, wife of the said Lawrence, as Lawrence had all the premises to himself and his assigns for life and the said Alice had a fourth part of the premises for life after Lawrence's death for her dower. The same was granted to them by the said Edmund Stevenson before the court. Fine 11s by the pledge of John Robinson of Goldshaie.

Lawrence Stevenson surrendered by Edmund Robinson, a tenant of the Queen, one messuage, other buildings, lands, tenements, meadows, grazing lands and pastures in le Fence in Goldshaiebothe in the Forest of Pendle, annual rent to the Queen 2s, now or lately in the tenure of Jane Stevenson, sister of the said Lawrence, to Richard, son of the said Lawrence, and his heirs for ever. Admittance sought. Christopher Hartley forbade fine by right of the said Lawrence and Alice, his wife, as Lawrence had all the premises to himself and his assigns for life and Alice had the fourth part of the premises for life after Lawrence's death for her dower. The same was granted to them by the said Richard Stevenson in open court. Fine 2s by the pledge of Edmund Robinsone.

Nicholas Robinson of Rougheley, junior, surrendered by Nicholas Robinson, greave of Pendle, one barn and 9½ acres of land, meadow, grazing land and pasture in a close of land called Great Intacke in the Forest of Pendle, annual rent to the Queen 2s 4d, to John Hargreaves of Barrowford and Nicholas Robinson, senior, as feofees according to an indenture made by (1) the said Nicholas Robinson, junior, and (2) Allen Carr of Capilsyd in the county of York dated 23rd March 13 Elizabeth I [1570/1]. Admittance sought and granted. Fine 2s 4d by the pledge of James Hargreaves.

[Membrane 2d]

Richard Hertley of Whiteleyhaieboith, a tenant of the Queen, surrendered one messuage and other buildings, lands, meadows, grazing lands, pastures and mosses in Wheitleyhaieboith in the Forest of Pendle, annual rent to the Queen 13s 3d, which Richard Verley, surviving feofee of Peter Verley, deceased, delivered to him, to the said Richard Verley and his heirs for ever. Admittance sought and granted. Fine 13s 4d by the pledge of Christopher Hartley of Haybothe.

James Browne, surviving feofee of Lawrence Hargreaves, deceased, surrendered by John Hargreaves of Goldshaie, a tenant of the Queen, one messuage, other buildings, lands, tenements, meadows, grazing lands, pastures and mosses in Whithaulghe and Rougheleigh in the Forest of Pendle, annual rent to the Queen 9s 3d, to Robert Hargreaves and his heirs for ever. Admittance sought and granted. Fine 9s 3d by the pledge of Geoffrey Hargreaves.

James Robinson, a tenant of the Queen, surrendered one messuage and other buildings, lands, tenements, meadows, grazing lands and mosses in Rougheleigh in the Forest of Pendle, annual rent to the Queen 8s 4d, which Richard Bybbie delivered to him, to Marion, wife of Christopher Verley, and the heirs of her body lawfully begotten, and in default of such issue remainder thereof to the right heirs of the said Richard Bybby for ever. Admittance sought and granted. Fine 8s 4d by the pledge of Nicholas Robinson.

Sum of this halmote £4 10d.

Sum of the said two halmotes of Penhull aforesaid £4 17s
Fines for land £4 10s; amercements 7s.
Approved and charged in the 13th year of Queen Elizabeth.

Colne

Halmote of the manor of Colne held there, Monday, 22nd January, 13 Elizabeth I [1570/1] before John Towneley, esq., chief steward there.

Inquisition taken there for the Queen to make enquiry upon the oaths of Thomas Emot, Edmund Ridihaulghe, John Walton, Nicholas Mitchell of Colne, William

Hanson, John Dryver, John Elott, John Robinson of Goldshay, John Hargreaves of Sabden, Robert Bawdwyne, James Willson, Gilbert Hartley of Swynden, Lawrence Rob't of Wynewall and James Mersden.

Henry Shawe was elected greave of Colne; John Ellot and John Forster were elected constables of Colne; Edmund Walton was elected constable of M'sden.

Henry Robinson alias Bunse[?] (12d) because he assaulted Henry Mankinhoiles.

Robert Hartley [*no amercement*] and Edmund Holgate (6d) because they assaulted each other.

Amercements 18d.

Barnard Hartley surrendered by Nicholas Mitchell of Colne, a tenant of the Queen, one parcel of land containing 12 feet in length and 12 feet in width in Colne on the south side of the house of John Blakey, now or lately in the tenure of Roger Blakey, clerk, to the said John Blakey, his heirs and assigns, for ever. Admittance sought. Christopher Robinson forbade fine by the right of the inheritance of Margaret Hartley, daughter of the said Barnard. John Blakey found pledge John Swayne to answer the forbid and was then admitted. Fine ½d by the pledge aforesaid.

[*Membrane 3*]

Forest of Trawden

Inquisition taken there for the Queen to make enquiry upon the oaths of Geoffrey Harteley of Trawden, Richard Shackilden of the same, Geoffrey Shackilden of the same, James Harteley, senior, of the same, Henry Harteley of the same, Robert Harteley of the same, Richard Harteley of the same, Lawrence Shuttleworth, James Harteley, junior, of Wynewall, John Dryver of the same, Roger Hardley [*sic*] of the same, Barnard Harteley of Wicolor, Christopher Harteley, junior, of the same, and Peter Harteley of the same.

James Harteley was elected greave of Trawden.

Thomas Mitton [*no amercement*] because he occupied one house, the inheritance of Richard Hartley, unjustly and contrary to the custom of the manor.

Lawrence Shuttleworth (2d) because he kept his fences open between his land and tenement and the land and tenement of Richard Hartley.

The said Lawrence Shuttleworth (2d) and John Dryver (2d) because they kept their fences open to the damage of their neighbours.

Amercements 6d.

Colne

At the halmote of the manor of Colne held there on 3rd December 10 Elizabeth I [1567] before the steward aforesaid, Nicholas Walker surrendered by

Henry Walton, late greave of Colne, three houses, three gardens, ½ an acre of land in Colne and one other ½ acre of land lying near le Vyver in Colne and also one other acre of land in Great Mersden, to Alexander Russheworth, gent., and his heirs for ever. Admittance sought. The said Nicholas Walker forbade fine by the right of his inheritance. The said Alexander found pledge James Foldes to answer the forbid and was then admitted. Fine 16d by the pledge of James Foldes.

At the halmote of the manor of Colne held there on 3rd December 10 Elizabeth I [1567] before the steward aforesaid, Henry Banester, gent., Richard Mytchell of Colne and John Hargreaves of Grenefeilde, (surviving feofees to the use of Nicholas Walker) surrendered (at the request of the said Nicholas) by Henry Walton, late greave of Colne, the same property as in the previous surrender to Alexander Russheworth, gent., and his heirs for ever. Admittance sought. Nicholas Walker forbade fine by the right of his inheritance. Alexander Russheworth found pledge James Folds to answer the forbid and was then admitted. Fine 16d by the pledge aforesaid.

Release. John Scale surrendered and for himself and his heirs released, remised and quit claimed into the Queen's hands all right, claim, title, estate, interest, possession and demand which he had or may have had in the future in all those messuages, lands, tenements, meadows, grazing lands and pastures in Colne now or lately in the tenure of John Robinson of Stanrod, to the said John Robinson and his heirs for ever. Admittance sought and granted. Fine 4d. [*Pledge not given*].

Sum of this halmote 5s ½d.

Colne
Halmote of the manor of Colne held there, Wednesday, 13th June, 13 Elizabeth I [1571] before John Towneley, esq., chief steward there.

Inquisition taken there for the Queen to make enquiry upon the oaths of Edward Mersden, John Blakey, senior, John Dryver, William Hanson, John Foldes, John Ellot, Christopher Dicconson, John Hargreaves of Ferneside, John Walton, Robert Bawdwyne, Robert Bulcocke, Henry Walton, John Mankinhoiles and Lawrence Willson.

Amercements 3s 4d.
Henry Tempeste of Broughton, gent., (excused 3s 4d) because he broke the Queen's ground and soil within the manor aforesaid.
The relict of Alexander Harste (6d) because she kept her fences open to the damage of her neighbours.
Amercements 14d.
The wife of Christopher Shore (4d) and Lawrence Breclif (4d) because they carried away four cartloads of stones out of the manor contrary to the custom.

One messuage and 2d of rent in Colne came into the Queen's hands by the death of William Mytton. Henry Mytton was his son and next heir and aged about fourteen years and Christopher Robinson was his guardian. Admittance was sought. Margaret, lately wife of the said William, forbade fine for her life and it was granted to her by the said Henry in open court. Fine 2d by the pledge of Henry Mankenhoiles.

Nicholas Mitchel died seised of one messuage and one garden in Colne. Edward Mytchell was his son and next heir and aged about thirty-nine weeks and John Cutler was his guardian. Admittance was sought. John Mytchell, brother of the said Nicholas Michell [sic], forbade fine by the right of his inheritance and John Scale forbade fine by the right of his inheritance. Edward Michell found pledges Henry Shawe and Robert Hartley to answer the forbids and admittance was then granted. Fine 4d by the pledges aforesaid.

[Membrane 3d]

John Hargreaves of Grenefeilde, Nicholas Mytchell and Richard Hergreaves (at the request of Jennet Hargreaves, widow, John Robinson of Goldshaie and James Hargreaves, son and heir apparent of the said John [sic]) surrendered by Henry Towneley, esq., a tenant of the Queen, two messuages and other buildings and 15 acres of land in Colne called Fearnyside, now or lately in the tenure of the said John Hargreaves and Richard Hargreaves, to Robert, son of Henry Shawe of Colne, Thomas, son and heir apparent of John Robinson of Sabden, John Cronckeshay, son and heir apparent of Leonard Cronckeshaie of West Close, and Thomas, son and heir apparent of Robert Whitacar, as feofees according to indentures made by (1) the said John Hergreaves and (2) Thomas Whitacar of Holme, gent., and Robert, his son and heir, dated 30th September 12 Elizabeth I [1570]. Admittance sought and granted. Fine 5s by the pledge of John Swayne.

Richard Smythez, gent., deputy steward for John Towneley, esq., chief steward there, surrendered one messuage and other buildings and 5 acres of land in Colne, now or lately in the tenure of John Blakey, (which Henry Towneley of Barsyde, esq., delivered to him) to the said John Blakey and Alice, his wife, and their assigns according to the intent. Admittance sought and granted. Fine 3s 4d by the pledge of Henry Barcrofte, gent.

The intent was that John and Alice Blakey were to be seised of the property for their lives. After their deaths, their assigns were to be seised to the use of such son or sons lawfully begotten of their bodies as John Blakey should nominate or appoint for 21 years after the deaths of the said John and Alice. The said John and Alice and their son were to pay the yearly rent to the Queen and also 14s 2d yearly to the said Henry Towneley, his heirs and assigns.

Forest of Trawden

Inquisition taken there for the Queen to make enquiry upon the oaths of Geoffrey Shackleden of Trawden and the other jurors who said they had nothing to present because all was well.

Release. John Scale surrendered and for himself and his heirs released, remised and quit claimed into the Queen's hands all right, claim, title, estate, interest, possession and demand which he had or might have had in the future in all those lands, tenements, meadows, grazing lands and pastures in Colne now or lately in the tenure of James M'sden, to the said James Marsden and his heirs for ever. Admittance sought and granted. Fine 4d. [*Pledge not given*].

Sum of this court 13s 7d.

Sum of the two halmotes aforesaid 18s 7½d.
Colne 17s 9½d; fines for land 11s 9½d; amercements 6s.
Troden 10d; fines for land 4d; amercements 6d.
Approved and charged in the 13th year of Queen Elizabeth.

Halmote of the manor of Accrington held there, Wednesday, 17th January, 13 Elizabeth I [1570/1] before John Towneley, esq., chief steward there.

Rossendall

Inquisition taken there for the Queen to make enquiry upon the oaths of John Ormerod of Gambleside, George Dureden, Oliver Pillinge, Lawrence Nuttall, John Lorde als. Bolton, Dionysius Hauworth of Crawshaiebothe, senior, Oliver Assheworth, Dionysius Hauworth of Cunstableleigh, Richard Crawshaie, George Nuttall, Edmund Lache of Cowop, Francis Bridge of Musbury, Nicholas Russheton, gent., Edward Ryley, junior, Robert Hauworth, Richard Walmesley and George Ryley.

Richard Heye was elected greave of Rossindale; Nicholas Cunlyff was elected greave of Accrington New Hold.

John Lawe of Tunsted (20s) because he kept his fences open between the land and tenement of Robert Lord and Tunsted Heyes.

John Talyor (12d) because he encroached a certain parcel of the way leading by the water in Wulfinden contrary to the verdict of twelve jurors chosen, charged and sworn for determining the same way.
Amercements 21s.

Edward Talior of Musbury died seised of two messuages and other buildings and certain lands and tenements within Musbury Park in the Forest of Rossindale, annual rent to the Queen 32s 6d. Geoffrey Talyor was his son and next heir and of full age. Admittance sought and granted. Fine 32s 6d by the pledge of Christopher Nuttall.

[Membrane 4]

John Tattersall of Tunsteid died about the date of the last court seised of half of one messuage and other buildings, lands, meadows, grazing lands, pastures and mosses in Tunsteid, Sedges and Sowecloughe in the Forest of Rossindale, annual rent to the Queen 14s. John Tattersall was his son and next heir and was aged about five years. Christopher Nuttall, son of Ralph, was his guardian. Admittance sought and granted. Fine 14s by the pledge of Lawrence Nuttall.

The said John Tattersall died also seised in reversion of the other half of the said messuage, etc. in Tunsted, Sedges and Sowecloughe. And also in one other messuage, other buildings and lands, meadows, grazing lands, pastures and mosses in Wullfinden called Shawecloughe and Shawe Hills in the Forest aforesaid, annual rent to the Queen 5s 4d. Admittance was sought. Alice, relict of the late John Tattersall, senior, forbade fine for a certain term for which she had the premises. John Tattersall found pledge Lawrence Nuttall to answer the forbid and was then admitted. Fine 19s 4d by the pledge aforesaid.

Charles, son of John Hauworth, late of Crawshaieboth, deceased, surrendered one messuage, other buildings and certain lands, meadows, grazing lands and pastures in le Backside of Crydden in the Forest of Rossindale, annual rent to the Queen 20d, now or lately in the tenure of Robert Lange, and 1d of rent in Henheides, to Henry Hauworthe, his brother, and his heirs for ever. Admittance sought. Robert Lange forbade fine as he had the premises for a certain term of years. Henry Hauworth found pledge George Hargreaves to answer the forbid and was then admitted. Fine 21d by the pledge aforesaid.

Dionysius Hauworth of Crawshaieboth, junior, and Oliver Ormerod of the same, feofees (at the request of Charles, son of John Hauworth of Crawshaieboth, late deceased) surrendered one messuage and the third part of one other messuage and certain lands, meadows, grazing lands, pastures and mosses in Lawnd of Crydden in the Forest of Rossindale, containing the third part of Crydden, and the third part of a parcel of land called Calfs Heye, annual rent to the Queen 10s, now or lately in the tenure of Richard Mankinhoyles, Henry Hauworth, Richard Gregory, Miles Hole and Oliver Ormerod or their assigns, and 1d rent in Henheads, to the said Charles Hauworth and his heirs for ever. Admittance sought. Richard Mankinholes, Henry Hauworth, Richard Gregory, Miles Hole and Oliver Ormerod forbade fine for a certain term. Charles Hauworth found pledge Dionysius Hauworth to answer the forbid and was then admitted. Fine 10s by the pledge aforesaid.

Henry Hauworth, greave of Rossindale, surrendered one parcel of land, a parcel of a pasture called Henheds, annual rent to the Queen 1d, (which George Nuttall and Lawrence Nuttall delivered to him) to Francis Nuttall, brother of the said George and Lawrence, and his heirs for ever. Admittance sought and granted. Fine 1d by the pledge of the said Lawrence Nuttall.

John Nuttall of Newalheighe surrendered by Henry Hauworth, greave of Rossindale, half of one messuage and other buildings and half of one parcel of land, meadow, grazing land, pasture and moss in Cowopp in the Forest of Rossindale called Cradgheie, annual rent to the Queen 12d, now or lately in the tenure or occupation of Gilbert Hill, to George Nuttall, one of the sons of the said John, his heirs and assigns for ever. Admittance sought and granted. Fine 12d by the pledge of Henry Hauworth.

The said John Nuttall surrendered by Henry Hauworth, greave of Rossindale, the other half of the property to his son George for twenty-four years from the feast of St. Michael the Archangel [29th September] last before the date of this court. Admittance sought and granted. Fine 12d by the pledge of Henry Hauworth.

John Tattersall of Bacopp surrendered by Lawrence Nuttall, a tenant of the Queen, one barn, one parcel of land called Sowecloughe, the half of Bacopp More and certain turfs in Bacoppheye, viz, 'yearlye one daie wurke of turves to be gotten in Bacopphey' in the Forest of Rossindale, annual rent to the Queen 7s 6d, to James Tattersall, son of the said John, and his heirs for ever. Admittance sought and granted. Fine 7s 6d by the pledge of John Lord.

James Tattersall of Bacopp, senior, surrendered by Lawrence Nuttall, a tenant of the Queen, one messuage and other buildings and one parcel of land called Sowecloughe, one other parcel of land called le Holmes and the half of Bacopp More in the Forest of Rossindale, annual rent to the Queen 6s 10½d, to Roger Tattersall, son of the said James, and his heirs for ever. Admittance sought and granted. Fine 6s 10d [*sic*] by the pledge of John Tattersall.

Peter Birtwisill surrendered by Lawrence Nuttall, a tenant of the Queen, all his part of a close of land called Neweclosehead and a parcel of land called le Edge and one other parcel of land called Over Bankes within the Forest of Rossindale, annual rent to the Queen 20d, now or lately in the tenure of the said Peter and John Heape, to Thomas Hauworth of Dedwencloughe and his assigns for twelve years after the death of Isabel, lately relict of Alexander Hauworth, deceased. Annual rent to Peter Birtwisill and his heirs 5s. Admittance sought and granted. Fine 20d by the pledge of William Jenkinson.

At the request of Robert Banester and Ellen, his wife, Owen, son and heir of Simon Haydock of Hesandfourth, gent., and James Robt., feofees to the use of the said Ellen, along with the said Robert and Ellen, surrendered by John Woodroff, a tenant of the Queen, the third part of one messuage and other buildings and the third part of all those lands, tenements, meadows, grazing lands, pastures and mosses in Swynshaie, Donockeshaie als. Prymarose Syke, Henheads and Frerehill in the Forest of Rossindale, annual rent to the Queen 7s 4d, and the third part of ½d, now or lately in the several tenures of the said Robert and Ellen Banester, William Barcrofte and Mary Towneley, illegitimate daughter of Richard Towneley, late of Towneley, esq., deceased, and their assigns, to John Towneley of Towneley, esq., his heirs and assigns for ever. Admittance sought. Geoffrey Rusheton, gent., forbade fine for a certain parcel of the premises called Frerehill by right of his inheritance. John Towneley found pledge George Hargreaves to answer the forbid and was then admitted. Fine 7s 4½d [*sic*] by the pledge aforesaid.

Ralph Hauworth and Francis Nuttall, tenants of the Queen, surrendered three messuages, other buildings, lands, tenements, meadows, grazing lands and pastures in Wulfinden in the Forest of Rossindale, annual rent to the Queen 6s 4d, now or lately in the tenure of James Chadwick, Hugh Jackeson and Richard Hayward, which James Lorde als. Bolton delivered to them, to George Lorde, one of the sons of the said James, and his heirs for ever. Admittance sought by George Lorde als. Bolton and it was granted. Fine 6s 4d by the pledge of Francis Nuttall.

The intent was that James Lorde should occupy the property for life and after his death it was to go to George and his heirs for ever. In default of such issue it was to go to the right heirs of the said James Lord Bolton [*sic*] for ever. Provided that Richard Haiward named in the surrender should quietly occupy that house and those lands and tenements in his occupation for life, paying 3s 4d yearly to the said James Lord and his heirs.

Haslingden

Inquisition taken there of the Old Hold to make enquiry for the Queen upon the oaths of Francis Garside, gent., Robert Dureden, Hugh Fenton, Robert Gregory, Robert Heighe, Hugh Talyor, James Roithewell, John Heape, senior, John Kennyon, Thomas Ryley, Henry Ryley, Christopher Jackeson, Richard Aithaulghe, Nicholas Grymeshaw and George Birtwisill.

John Heape, junior, was elected greave of Haslingden; Ralph Tailior was elected constable of Haslingden; Thomas Garsyde and John Radcliff, junior, were elected appraisers; Robert Dureden and Robert Hey were elected fence lookers.

Lawrence Rawstorne of Haslingden (4d) and John Romesbothome (4d) because they kept and allowed wanderers and strangers in their houses in the night-time contrary to the statute.

Thomas Garsyde (2d), Charles Whitacar (2d) and Robert Hauworth (2d) for tracking hares in the snow contrary to the statute.

John Rydinge was elected constable [*crossed out*] greave of Huncote and Accrington Old Hold.

Lawrence Jackson and Richard Aitaulgh were elected appraisers, fence lookers and pounders.

Amercements 14d.

Haslingden

John Nuttall of Newalheighe surrendered by Adam Holden, greave of Haslingden, 2 acres of land in Haslingden, which he lately got from Hugh Garside of Ewoode, now or lately in the tenure of James Jackeson, to George, son of the said John Nuttall, and his heirs for ever. Admittance sought and granted. Fine 8d by the pledge of Adam Holden, gent.

Sum of this halmote £6 12s 2½d.

[Membrane 5]

Halmote of the manor of Accrington held there, Thursday, 14th June, 13 Elizabeth I [1571] before John Towneley, esq., chief steward there.

Rossendall

Inquisition taken there of the Forest for the Queen to make enquiry upon the oaths of Nicholas Rusheton, gent., Ellis Cunlyff, Edward Ryley, Edmund Pillinge, George Ryley, Thomas Duckeworth, Christopher Nuttowe, Lawrence Tailior, George Ormerod, George Dureden, Evan Assheworth, Oliver Pillinge, Richard Crawshaie, Dionysius Hauworth of Constableligh, Dionysius Hauworth, junior, Francis Nuttall, James Pyccopp and Edmund Lache.

Gilbert Lawe (6d) because he made an affray on Ottiwell Haworth.

John Bridge alias Jenken (6d) because he kept his fences open upon Rowtonstall Edg.

Amercements 12d.

Lawrence Holden and George Ryleye, were elected fence lookers in Accrington New Hold. Hugh Pillinge, Christopher Nuttall, George Ormerod, Richard Crawshaie and Lawrence Talyor were elected fence lookers in Rossindale.

At the halmote of the manor of Accrington held there Tuesday, 6th November, 7 Elizabeth I [1565] before the steward aforesaid, Richard Rawstorne of Wulfindenboth surrendered by Lawrence Nuttall, then greave of Rossindale, one messuage and other buildings and one parcel of land in Wulfindenboith, Wulfinden and Henheads in the Forest of Rossindale, annual rent to the Queen 15s 6½d ¼d, now or lately in the tenure of the said Richard Rawstorne and Richard Crawshaie or their assigns, to Christopher Tattersall and Jennet, his wife, and their assigns for twenty-one years after the deaths of Richard Rawstorne of le Lome[1], father of the said Richard, and Ellen Rawstorne, widow, mother of the said Richard Rawstorne of le Lome. Admittance sought. Richard Crawshaie forbade fine by right of Agnes, his wife, for her dower. Christopher and Jennet Tattersall allowed the forbid in open court and were then admitted. An annual rent of 15s 6½d ¼d at the feast of St. James the Apostle [25th July] was payable to Richard and Ellen Rawstorne and their heirs during the term. Fine 15s 6½d ¼d by the pledge of John Nuttall.

Dionysius Hauworth, a tenant of the Queen, surrendered one messuage and other buildings, lands, meadows, grazing lands, pastures and mosses in Wulfinden

---

[1] Lumb Hall, Edenfield

and Henheads in the Forest of Rossindale, annual rent to the Queen 2s 2d, now or lately in the tenure of Peter Crabtrye, which Lawrence Rawstorne, gent., delivered to him, to Edward, son of the said Lawrence, and Lawrence, son of the said Edward, and their heirs for ever. Admittance sought and granted. Fine 4s 4d [sic] by the pledge of Ralph Nuttowe.

Dionysius Hauworth, a tenant of the Queen, surrendered one messuage and other buildings, lands, meadows, grazing lands and pastures in Rowcliff Woode in the Forest of Rossindale, annual rent to the Queen 16s 8d, now or lately in the tenure of Thomas Bridge, which Lawrence Rawstorne, gent., delivered to him, to Edward, son of the said Lawrence, and Lawrence, son of the said Edward, and their heirs for ever. Admittance sought and granted. Fine 33s 4d [sic] by the pledge of Ralph Nuttowe.

John Walton and Elizabeth, his wife, surrendered by Lawrence Nuttall, a tenant of the Queen, one messuage and other buildings, lands, meadows, grazing lands, pastures and mosses in Wulfindenboith, Wulfinden and Henheads in the Forest of Rossindale, annual rent to the Queen 7s 9d, now or lately in the tenure of Giles Hole and his assigns, to John, son of Oliver Halsted of Roweley, John, son of John Nutter of Pendle, John, son of Lawrence Nuttall, and Richard, son and heir apparent of Oliver Ormerod of Wulfinden, and their heirs for ever as feofees according to the intent. Admittance sought and granted. Fine 7s 9d by the pledge of Oliver Ormerod of Wulfinden.

The intent was that the feofees were to be seised of the property to the use of the said Giles Hole and Elizabeth, his wife, and their assigns for life. After their deaths, the feofees were to be seised to the use of such person or persons nominated by the said Giles for twenty-one years. Giles and Elizabeth Hole and any other person occupying the property were to pay not only the rent to the Queen, but also an annual rent of 7s 9d to John Walton and his heirs.

John Walton and Elizabeth, his wife, surrendered by Lawrence Nuttall, a tenant of the Queen, one messuage, other buildings, lands, tenements, meadows, grazing lands, pastures and mosses in Wulfindenboith, Frerehill and Henheds in the Forest of Rossindale, annual rent to the Queen 6s 8½d ¼d and half of ¼d, now or lately in the tenure of Richard Hargreaves and his assigns, to John, son of Oliver Halsted of Roweley, John, son of John Nutter of Pendle, John, son of Lawrence Nuttall of Newalhey, and Richard, son and heir apparent of Oliver Ormerod of Wulfinden, and their heirs for ever as feofees according to the intent. Admittance sought and granted. Fine 6s 8d [sic] by the pledge of John Taylior.

[Membrane 5d]

The intent was that the feofees were to be seised of the property to the use of the said Richard Hargreaves and Alice, his wife, for life. After their deaths, the feofees were to be seised to the use of such person or persons nominated by the said Richard for twenty-one years. Richard and Alice Hargreaves and any other person occupying the property were to pay not only the rent to the Queen, but also an annual rent of 6s 8½d ¼d and half of ¼d to John Walton and his heirs.

John Hauworth of Wulfinden, junior, and Elizabeth, his wife, surrendered by Henry Hauworth, greave of Rossindale, one messuage and other buildings, lands, meadows, grazing lands, pastures and mosses in Wulfinden in the Forest of Rossindale, annual rent to the Queen 3s 2d, to Oliver Ormerod of Wulfinden, his heirs and assigns for ever. Admittance sought and granted. Fine 3s 2d by the pledge of Gilbert Lawe.

Afterwards Oliver Ormerod resurrendered the property to John Hauworth for life, with remainder thereof to the right heirs of the bodies of the said John and Elizabeth, his wife, for ever. Admittance sought. Thurstan Boithe forbade fine by the right of Alice, his wife, for her dower. John Hauworth found pledge Edward Ingham to answer the forbid and was then admitted. Fine 3s 2d by the pledge aforesaid.

Accrington New Hold

Oliver Ormerod of Wulfinden surrendered by Robert Ryley, a tenant of the Queen, one parcel of land called Migehaulgh in Cowhowses in the Forest of Rossindale, annual rent to the Queen 8d, now or lately in the tenure of Ralph Walmesley, to John Ormerod of Huncote and his heirs for ever. Admittance sought and granted. Fine 8d by the pledge of John Birtwisill.

Gilbert Russheton surrendered by Geoffrey Russheton, greave of Accrington, one messuage and other buildings, lands, meadows, grazing lands, pastures and mosses called Antley containing the third part of the 'vaccarie' of Antley in Accrington New Hold in the Forest of Rossindale, annual rent to the Queen 60s, to Robert, son of the said Gilbert Russheton, and his heirs for ever. Admittance sought. The said Gilbert forbade fine as he had all the property for life and also because he reserved to himself sufficient dower of the premises for the woman who was his wife at the death of his death. This was granted to him in open court by the said Robert Russheton who was then admitted. Fine 60s by the pledge of Geoffrey Russheton.

Rossindale

The following surrenders were enrolled verbatim on the advice of Francis Samwell, esq., the Queen's auditor, at the request of Oliver Birtwisill, gent., in the manner and form they were presented in this court by the oaths of James Wamesley and Robert Ryley, tenants of the Queen.

[*The two surrenders are enrolled in English.*]

This surrender made the 21st day of November in the year of our Lord God a thousand, five hundred, threescore and eight [1568] in the tenth year of the reign of our sovereign lady the Queen, &c. Unto this halmote is come Alexander Ryley of Highe Ryley within the Forest of Rossindale by James Walmesley and Robert Ryley and doth surrender into the hands of our sovereign lady the Queen the half of one messuage with other buildings with Henhards in Highe Ryley, now in the tenure of me the said Alexander Ryley, to the yearly rent of thirteen shillings five pence halfpenny farthing, to the use of Mabel, my wife during her widowhood, to remain to my son and heir apparent Raynolde, and his heirs for ever. Provided always that if it fortune Mable, my wife, to die within the space of twenty-four years after the date hereof, that then the fruits and profits of one noble's[1] worth being now in the tenure of me the said Alexander to remain to my daughter, Jane, during the term of twenty-four years after the date hereof if she keeps herself unmarried. The remainder to my son, Raynolde, and his heirs for ever.

[*In the margin*] He was admitted, a fine. Fine 13s 15½d.

The surrender made the 21st day of November in the year of our Lord God a thousand, five hundred, threescore and eight [1568] in the tenth year of the reign of our sovereign lady the Queen, &c. Unto this halmote is come Alexander Ryley of Highe Ryley within the Forest of Rossindale by James Wallmesley and Robert Ryley and doth surrender into the hands of our sovereign lady the Queen the other half of the same messuage with other buildings with Henhards in Highe Ryley in the Forest of Rossindale, now in the tenure of Alice Ryley, late wife of Randle Ryley, to the yearly [rent *omitted*] of thirteen shillings five pence halfpenny farthing, to the use of myself during my life and to my three daughters, Alice, Jennet and Isabel, for twenty years after the date hereof. Provided always that if it fortune any of the said daughters to be married or die, the fruits and profits to remain to the other sisters or sister until the end of the twenty years. At the end of the term, remainder to Raynolde, my son.

[*In the margin*]He was admitted, a fine. Fine 13s 5½d.

These being witnesses, James Birtwisill, Thomas Ryley, George Ryley and Roger Cowopp. Memorandum that the above named Alice, late wife of Randale Ryley, forbade the last recited fine upon the admittance of the same, that she might have the lands, tenements and hereditaments in the same comprised during her natural life. And the three sisters above named for their pledge found Thomas Ryley and James Walmesley to answer the said Alice according to the custom of the manor of Accrington.

[*Membrane 6*]

At the halmote of the manor of Accrington held there Saturday, 10th March, 13 Elizabeth I [1570/1] before John Towneley, esq., chief steward there, by virtue of the Queen's letters or commission sent to the same John Towneley. The tenor of which letters follows in these words:

[*In English*] Elizabeth, by the grace of God, of England, France and Ireland, Queen, Defender of the Faith, &c. To our trusty and well beloved John Towneley, esq., our steward of our manor or lordship of Accrington, parcel of our Duchy of Lancaster,

---

[1] A noble was a gold coin worth 6s 8d (half a mark).

in our county of Lancaster, greeting. Whereas Ralph Russheton of Dunkenhaulghe in our county of Lancaster, esq., hath exhibited his bill of complaint to our Chancellor and Council of our Duchy in our Duchy Chamber at our Palace of Westminster, showing by the same that whereas one John Rysheton, late of Dunkenhaulghe aforesaid, was lawfully seised by copy of court roll according to the custom of the said manor of Accrington of and in reversion of one water corn mill called Accrington Milne situate and being in Accrington in the said county of Lancaster after the decease of Ellen Rissheton, wife of Henry Rissheton, esq., deceased, who did hold the same for term of her life, and that he being so thereof seised, as well in consideration of great sums of money as also for divers other good considerations him moving, did together with the said Ellen Rissheton, surrender the same mill according to the custom of our said manor into the hands of the then greave of our said manor, to the use of the said Ralph and his heirs. And that the said surrender, either through the default of the said greave or else by oversight of the clerk who entered the same, the name of the said John Ryssheton was omitted and left out of the same surrender and the name of the said Ellen Ryssheton was only entered in the same, where indeed the said original surrender was made to the said greave by them both and in both their names as the said Ralph in his bill alleges that he is able to prove as well by the said greave who did present the same as also by divers witnesses which were present as well at the conclusion and agreement had between the said Ralph and the said John and Ellen for the same as also at the making of the said surrender by the said John and Ellen to the said greave to the use of the said Ralph as is aforesaid as by the same bill of complaint remaining in our said Duchy Chamber more plainly appeareth. We therefore considering the premises, minding to understand the truth therein, and entrusting in your wisdom and discretion, will and require you at time convenient by you to be limited and appointed calling before you by virtue hereof the said Ralph Rissheton and John Rissheton to repair yourself to our said manor of Accrington and then and there to summon a court and call before you twenty-four of our copyholders and customary tenants according to the custom of our said manor and thereupon to swear and impanel them truly to inquire and present whether the said surrender was made by the said John Rissheton and Ellen, or but only by the said Ellen or not, and thereupon if your doings and proceedings in the premises together with the verdict so to be taken by you herein as aforesaid to certify our Chancellor and Council of our said Duchy in our said Duchy Chamber by your writings enclosed under you seal with their own letters in the Quindene of Easter next coming, not failing hereof as we trust you. Given at our said Palace under the seal of our said Duchy the 25th day of November in the 13th year of our reign [1570].

Inquisition taken there to enquire upon the articles in the commission aforesaid specified, viz by the oaths of Hugh Halsted, gent., Richard Pollard, Robert Whitacar, Francis Webster, Lawrence Whitacar, Ellis Robinson, John Tailyor, John

Walton, John Swayne, John Dryver, John Foldes, John Hergreaves, John Harryson, John Dugdale of le Standes, Richard Hoole, Christopher Migecocke, John Woulton, John Moore, Francis Garside, gent., Adam Holden, gent., Robert Dureden, John Kennyon, Thomas Ryley and Christopher Jackeson who said that John Rissheton and Ellen Rissheton, mother of the said John Ryssheton, jointly surrendered the mill called Accrington Mylne to the use of Ralph Ryssheton and his heirs.

[Membrane 6d]

[Blank]

[Membrane 7]

Christopher Romesbothome complained against Edmund Romesbotheyme of Okenheadwood in a plea of a broken agreement whereof the same Christopher suffered damage to the value of £20. The defendant denied the charge. The jury of Edmund Assheworthe of Wulfindenboth, Robert Assheworth of the same, John Wulfinden, James Tattersall of Dedwynecloughe, Christopher Bridge of the same, George Dureden, Christopher Cronckshaie, Francis Bridge, James Pyccopp of Wulfinden, George Nuttall, John Birtwisill and Edmund Lache found that the said Edmund Romesbothome broke and did not carry out the agreement made by him and the plaintiff and was therefore in mercy. Amercement 2d.

Henry Hauworthe of Constableleighe complained against John Assheworth of the same in a plea of trespass because the defendant blocked and stopped up one way between the plaintiff's capital messuage and a certain parcel of land of the plaintiff's called Reids contrary to ancient use and custom and contrary to the custom of the manor. The jury of George Dureden, Gilbert Birtwisill, Christopher Bridge, John Wulfinden, Peter Birtwisill, Hugh Pilling, Richard Crawshaie, Edmund Lache, James Walm'sley, Richard Walm'sley, Edward Tailior of Musbury and Francis Bridge of Musburye found that the defendant had stopped up the way and was therefore in mercy. Amercement 2d.

Henry Hauworthe of Constableleigh complained against John Assheworthe of the same in a plea of trespass because the defendant had used a path called in English 'a fote waie' through a parcel of the plaintiff's land called Reids contrary to ancient use and the custom of the manor. The jury of George Dureden and the other jurors found that the defendant had used the way and was therefore in mercy. Amercement 2d.

Peter Byrtwisill of Dedwencloughe complained against John Bridge of Sedewast in a plea of trespass because the defendant had illegally and contrary to the custom of the manor used a certain way through the plaintiff's land and tenement in le Graystone Dole contrary to ancient use and where he had no right, whereof the plaintiff had suffered damage to the value of 40s. The jury of John Ormerod alias Lodge, George Ormerod, Robert Assheworthe of Fernes, George Dureden, James Hauworthe of Crawshaieboth, Hugh Heighe, Oliver Romesbothome of Okenheadwood, Ralph Hauworth, Evan Assheworth

85

[Assheworth *crossed out*] Scofield, James Assheworthe of Lenches, William Tailior of Wulfinden and Edmund Assheworthe alias Cheken found that the defendant ought to use the said way and that the plaintiff was in mercy for a false plea. Amercement 2d.

Peter Byrtwisill of Dedwencloughe complained against John Bridge of Sedewast in a plea of partition made not only of the ground in le Neweclose but also of the fences there between the plaintiff and the defendant with metes and bounds according to the custom of the manor. The defendant denied holding any lands or fences in Neweclose. The jury of John Ormerod alias Loidg, George Ormerod and the other jurors said that they had made a division and partition of the lands and fences as was clear by the metes and bounds put in place by them. Therefore the plaintiff was in mercy. Amercement 2d.

James Lorde of Bolton[*sic*], by John Lorde, his son, and with the said John Lorde and Christopher Bridge, complained against James Lorde of Bacopp, John Tattersall and Lawrence Rawstorne, gent., in a plea of trespass because the defendant blocked and stopped up one usual way between Bacopp and one close of land called Calfscoteleighe. The jury of Robert Assheworth of Fernes, John Wulfinden, James Tattersall of Dedwencloughe, Henry Kirshaie, Edmund Lache of Cowopp, George Dureden of Lovecloughe, Gilbert Birtwisill of the same, Oliver Romesbothome, Edward Talyor of Musbury, Evan Scofeild and Edmund Assheworth alias Chekyne found that the defendants had obstructed the way contrary to ancient use and custom of the manor and were therefore in mercy. Amercement 2d.

Sum of this halmote £13 3s 6½d ¼d.

Sum of the two halmotes aforesaid £14 15s 9¼d
Rossendale £11 13s 3¼d; fines for land £10 10s 3¼d, amercements 23s
Haslingden 22d; fines for land 8d, amercements 14d
Accrington New Hold 60s 8d total of fines for land
Approved and charged in the 13th year of Queen Elizabeth.

Ightenhill
Halmote of the manor of Ightenhill held at Bruneley, Friday, 12th January, 13 Elizabeth I [1570/1] before John Towneley, esq., chief steward there.

William Whipp (excused) because he made an affray upon John Hey.
William Collyson (12d) and John Robinson (12d) because they made an affray on each other and because the said John drew blood on the said William.
John Heye (12d) because he kept and maintained strangers in his house.
Robert Roo (6d) because he received into his house a woman vagrant who now lives with him as a servant.

James Whithead (12d) and Thomas Fletcher (12d) because they made an affray together.

Thomas Boithe (12d) because he received a woman stranger whom he looked after as if he kept an inn contrary to the form of the statute.

Amercements 6s 6d.

William Hertley (12d) and Lawrence Willson (2d) because they kept unlawful ways between Mylsyke and Rydyford.

John Hargreaves of Lomisley (12d) because he kept an illegal way between his house and Whitfeild.

Anne Towneley, widow, (12d) because she made a rescue upon the greave in the execution of his office for the Queen.

John Pollard of Bruneley (2d) because he took in an unknown woman called 'banester wife'.

Charles Gryme (excused) because he kept and maintained vagabonds and vagrants.

James Leighe (4d) and his wife because they kept illegal games in their house.

John Hanson (4d) and Alexander Gryme (4d) because they did not grind their corn and grain at the Queen's mill.

Geoffrey, son of John Robinson of Haberghameves (4d), William Cocker (4d), William, son of Alexander Ryley (4d), James, son of George Ryley (4d), and Edmund Lee (4d) because they played at cards in 'Iansons howse.'

Amercements 2s 8d.

Whereas a penalty of 20s was imposed at the last halmote that Anne Towneley, widow, (20s), lately wife of Nicholas Towneley, esq., deceased, should lay open one usual and ancient way through the land and tenement in her tenure called Roylhill before the date of this halmote which she refused to do and so far had not done.

Amercement 20s.

George Ryley and Margaret, his wife, surrendered by John Towneley, esq., chief steward, seven selions of land called in English 'rigges or landes' in Bruneley in a close of land called le Towneoldefeilde containing 2 acres, to William Barcrofte of Barcrofte and John Smythe and their assigns for the lives of the said George and Margaret Ryley, the said term to start after a term that John Turner of Padiham had in the premises. Admittance sought and granted. Fine 8d by the pledge of Barnerd Towneley.

John Fletcher alias Cardmaker, son and heir of William Fletcher alias Cardmaker of Bruneley, 'laborer', surrendered by John Towneley, esq., chief steward there, and in return for £18 paid by Thomas Towneley of Grenefeilde in the county of Lancaster, gent., all those messuages, lands, tenements, meadows, grazing lands and pastures in Bruneley containing 28 acres, now or lately in the tenure of the said Thomas Towneley and Geoffrey Wilkinson or their assigns. And also the said John Fletcher alias Cardmaker remised, released and quit claimed for himself and his heirs all right, etc. which he had or might have had in the future in the premises to the said Thomas Towneley and Lucy, his wife, for ever. Admittance sought and granted. Fine 6s 8d by the pledge of Barnerd Towneley.

Afterwards the said Thomas Towneley and Lucy, his wife, surrendered by Nicholas Harger, a tenant of the Queen, one croft called Wyllcrofte containing 8 falls of land, one close called Longeholme containing 7½ roods of land, one close called Lonye Banck containing 6 roods 5 falls, one close called Deenyrode containing 6½ roods 9 falls, one parcel of land called Wheat Pighill containing ½ a rood 14 falls, one parcel called Newerode containing 6½ roods and one other parcel lying on the south side of le Stubbinge Medowe containing 34 falls of land, to Henry Taylyor and his heirs for ever. Admittance sought and granted. Fine 2s 8d by the pledge of John Taylior.

The same people surrendered, remised and released by Nicholas Harg', a tenant of the Queen, one close called Rappocke Rode containing 10½ roods 10 falls and one close called Stubbinge containing 4 roods 9 falls in Bruneley, now or lately in the tenure of the said Thomas Towneley, to John Talior of le Cloughe and his heirs for ever. Admittance sought and granted. Fine 2s 8d by the pledge of Henry Tailyor.

The same people surrendered one house with other buildings and one close of land near adjoining the said house and one house late in the tenure of Geoffrey Wilkinson with one barn beneath le Holme of a certain Richard Woodroff containing 13 roods 6 falls. Also 13½ roods of land called Heleyrode, 5 roods of land, except 10 falls, lying on the 'northestsyde' of a close called Newerode, and a way to carry and recarry with his carts, waggons and other carriages and for all other necessary purpose through a close called Longeholme and through Lamebank in Bruneley, to Peter Cloughe and his heirs for ever. Admittance sought and granted. Fine 2s 8d by the pledge of John Talyor.

Thomas Willysell and Ingram, his son, surrendered by John Houghton, a tenant of the Queen, two closes called Shepecote Heys containing 6 acres, a parcel of le Scolebanke, now or lately in the tenure of Christopher Dudgshone and Richard Shorrocke of Padiham, to the said Christopher and Richard and their assigns for six years from the feast of the Purification of the Blessed Virgin Mary next [2nd February]. Admittance sought and granted. Fine 2s by the pledge of Lawrence Whitacar of Padiham.

William Halsted of Banckehowse surrendered by John Woodroff, a tenant of the Queen, one messuage and other buildings, meadows, grazing lands, and pastures in Bruneley called Banckehowse containing 17½ acres of land, now or lately in the tenure of the said William Hallsted and his assigns, to Evan Haydocke of Hesandforthe, gent., John, son of Oliver Hallsted of Roweley, Edmund, son of Richard Tattersall of Brerecliff, and John, son of the said John Woodroff, and their heirs as feofees according to the intent. Admittance sought and granted. Fine 5s 10d by the pledge of John Woodroff, senior.

The intent was that the feofees were to be seised of the property to the use of the said William Halsted and his assigns for life. After his death, they were to be seised to the uses given in his last will and testament.

Ingram Willysell of Scolebancke surrendered by Robert Roe, a tenant of the Queen, one close or parcel of land, late parcel of one close called le Great Feilde, previously divided from the same close, containing 6 acres in Padiham, now or lately in the tenure of Thomas Shutleworth, son of Hugh Shotleworthe of Galthropp, to the said Thomas Shutleworth and his assigns for six years from the feast of the Annunciation of the Blessed Virgin Mary [25th March] in the twelfth year of the reign of our lady Elizabeth now Queen [1570]. Admittance sought and granted. Fine 2s by the pledge of Hugh Shutleworth, gent.

Robert Ingham of Fullage, John Whitacar of Myclehurste, Robert Whitacar of Heley, and Robert Towne, feofees of Richard Ingham of Bruneleywod, (at the request of the said Richard), surrendered by John Tat'sall, greave of Ightenhill, one messuage and 18½ acres of land in Bruneleywood to the said Richard, his heirs and assigns, for ever. Admittance sought and granted. Fine 6s 2d by the pledge of Robert Ingeham of Fullage.

Afterwards, the said Richard Ingham surrendered one messuage, other buildings and 15 acres of land, viz all the lands, tenements and hereditaments which 'he hayth lyinge benethe the lone in Bruneleywood', to John, son of Robert Ingham of Fullage, William Barcroft, son of Robert Barcroft, Henry, son of William Barcrofte of Swynden, and Nicholas, son of James Bancrofte, and their heirs as feofees according to indentures made by (1) the said Richard Ingham and (2) Stephen Saiger of Cliveg' dated 13th October 9 Elizabeth I [1567]. Admittance sought and granted. Fine 6s by the pledge of Robert Ingham.

[Membrane 8]

William Barcrofte of Barcrofte, John Hallstede of Windlehowse and Robert Hallsted (at the request of Christopher Riddihaulghe lately of Hensall and Robert, his son,) surrendered by Christopher Whitacar, greave of Ightenhill, the third part of all their customary messuages, lands and tenements in Higheriddihaulghe within the jurisdiction of this court containing 2½ acres and the third part of half of 1 acre now or lately in the tenure of William Hallsted, son of John Halsted alias Leis, and his assigns, to John Parker of Extwisill, gent., and John Halstede, son of John Halsted of Wyndlehowse, and their heirs as feofees not only according to indentures made by (1) the said Christopher Riddihaulgh and Robert, his son, and (2) the said William Halsted dated 24th December 11 Elizabeth I [1568], but also according to the intent. Admittance sought and granted. Fine 21d by the pledge of Hugh Halsted, gent.

The intent was that the feofees were to be seised of the property to the use of the said Christopher Riddihaulghe for life, and after his death to the use of Robert, his eldest son, and his heirs for ever. Provided always that this intent did not hinder the said William Halsted or his assigns in their enjoyment of any commodity, covenant or article limited unto him by the said indentures.

The same people surrendered by Christopher Whitacar, greave of Ightenhill, the third part of all their customary messuages, lands and tenements in Higheriddihaulghe containing 2½ acres and the third part of half of 1 acre of land, now or lately in the tenure of John Wyndle, son of William Windle late of Higheryddihaulghe, or his assigns, to John Parker of Extwisill, gent., and John, son of John Halsted of Wyndlehowse, and their heirs as feofees not only according to indentures made by (1) the said Christopher and Robert Riddihaulghe and (2) the said John Wyndle dated 24th December 11 Elizabeth I [1568], but also according to the intent. Admittance sought and granted. Fine 21d by the pledge of Hugh Halsted.

The intent was that the feofees were to be seised of the property to the use of the said Christopher Ryddihaulghe for life, and after his death to the use of Robert Riddihaulghe and his heirs for ever. The intent was not to hinder the said John Windle or his assigns in their enjoyment of any profit, commodity, covenant or article limited unto him by the said indentures.

Sum of this halmote 72s 6d.

Halmote of the manor of Ightenhill held at Bruneley, Thursday, 7th June 13 Elizabeth I [1571] before John Towneley, chief steward there.

Inquisition taken there for the Queen to make enquiry upon the oaths of Hugh Halsted, gent., Francis Webster, Robert Houghton, Lawrence Whitacar of Highe Whitacar, John Whitacar of Miclehurste, Robert Whitacar of Heley, John Tattersall, Thomas Boithe, Robert Towne, senior, John Swayne, William Lund, James Folds, John Hargreaves of Lomyshaie, John Robinson of Oldland, Richard Aycroid and Richard Tattersall.

Anne Towneley was elected greave of Ightenhill.

The relict of the late William Fletcher (6d) because she took in and kept strangers and vagabonds.

Edmund Leye (12d) because he took in divers people (in certain cottages built upon his land and tenement) to his neighbours' bad example.

John Grenewood (4d) because he got turfs upon Bruneley More contrary to the bye-laws.

James Tattersall (2d) and William Hancocke [no amercement] did likewise. Amercements 2s.

George Nowell was elected constable of Bruneley.

Alexander Willson (12d) because he took in and kept vagrants and strangers.

John Pollard (2d) did likewise.

Robert Hodshone (6d) because he took in and kept a mistress in his house.

Thomas Whitwhame (8d) because he took in and kept vagabonds and vagrants.

Robert Hergreaves of Lomeshaie (8d) because he did not repair and make in a sufficient manner one way within his land and tenement.

The relict of the late William Hancocke (4d) because she trespassed on the common pasture of Padiham.

Nicholas Cockeshot was elected constable of Padiham.

Miles Smythe (12d) and his wife because they cheated stranger boys and servants of their parents' and masters' fruits and corn.

Nicholas Billington (12d) and Ingram Willycell (12d) because they fished with nets during the night.

Edmund, son of John Robinson of Old Laund, Ellis Robinson, and James, son of Nicholas Robinson (at the request of Jennet Hargreaves, widow, John Hargreaves of Goldshaw, and James, son and heir apparent of the said John) surrendered by John Robinson of Old Land, a tenant of the Queen, one messuage, other buildings and 18 acres in Padiham and 1d of rent in Sabden banck, now or lately in the tenure of John Tattersall, William Whitacar, John Merser, Christopher Dodshone and Thomas Loneisdale, to Robert, son of Henry Shawe of Colne, John, son and heir apparent of John Robinson of Sabden, John, son and heir apparent of Leonard Cronckeshaie of Westclose, and Thomas, son and heir apparent of Robert Whitacar, and their heirs as feofees according to an indenture made by (1) the said John Hargreaves and (2) Thomas Whitacar of Holme, gent., and Robert, his son and heir apparent, dated 30th September 12 Elizabeth I [1570]. Admittance sought and granted. Fine 6s by the pledge of Ellis Robinson.

[Membrane 8d]

Lawrence Whitacar of Highe Whitacar, gent., surrendered by Ellis Robinson of Padiham, a tenant of the Queen, 6 acres of oxgang land in le westend of Padiham, now or lately in the tenure of Margaret, relict of the late Nicholas Rob't of Symondstone, and her assigns, to the said Margaret and her children for the life of the said Lawrence Whitacar. Admittance sought and granted. Fine 20d [*crossed out*] 2s by the pledge of Lawrence Whitacar of Padiham.

Peter Cloughe surrendered one house now or lately in the tenure of the relict of the late Miles Rob't and one house newly built and half of one barn and half of one garden lying in le Holme containing 6½ roods and 3 falls of land. And also 6½ roods and the fourth part of 1 rood called Heleyrode. And likewise 2½ roods [*blank*] part of 10 falls of land lying on 'le northestsyde' of a close called le Newerod. And one sufficient way to carry and recarry with his carts and waggons and for all other necessary purposes through le Longe Holme and Lamebancke in Bruneley, to Henry Sager and his assigns for twenty-one years from the feast of the Invention of the Holy Cross [3rd May] last. Admittance sought and granted. An annual rent of 8s 9d was payable to Peter Cloughe. Fine 20d by the pledge of John Tattersall. Let it be remembered that Agnes, wife of Peter Cloughe, was examined and confessed alone by the steward and said she was not compelled but acted from her own free will.

The said Peter Cloughe and Agnes, his wife, surrendered one house newly built in Bruneley, now or lately in the tenure of Henry Sager, to the said Henry and his assigns for nineteen years immediately after the twenty-one years granted to the said Henry by the last surrender. Admittance sought and granted. Fine 20d [crossed out] ½d by the pledge of John Tattersall.

Peter Cloughe and Agnes, his wife, surrendered one house lately in the tenure of John Hutchyon and half of one barn and half of one garden lying in le Holme containing 6½ roods 3 falls. Also 6½ roods and the fourth part of 1 rood called Heleyrode. And likewise 2½ roods and [blank] part of 10 falls of land in the north-east side of a close called le Newerod. And one sufficient way to carry and recarry with his carts and waggons and for all other necessary purposes through le Longe Holme and Lamebancke in Bruneley, to John Turner and his assigns for twenty-one years from the feast of the Invention of the Holy Cross [3rd May] last. Admittance sought and granted. An annual rent of 5s 5d was payable to Peter Cloughe. Fine 20d by the pledge of John Tattersall.

Whereas a penalty of 20s was imposed at the last court that Anne Towneley (20s), widow, lately wife of Nicholas Towneley, esq., deceased, should lay open one way used since ancient times through her land and tenement called Roylhill before the date of this court which she refused to do and so far had not done to the grave damage of her neighbours.

At the halmote of the manor of Ightenhill held at Bruneley, Wednesday, 10th December 11 Elizabeth I [1568] before the steward aforesaid, it was presented by the oaths of Nicholas Harger, John Whitacar of Miclehurste, William Foldes, Robert Roo, John Robinson of Goldshaie, John Hargreaves, John Higgyn, Henry Willysell, Richard Tattersall, William Smythe of Hill, John Hallsted of Windlehowse, William Loynde, senior, Francis Webster and George Smythe of Hollyngreave that Henry Walton of Barkerhowse died seised of half of one acre of land in Little M'sden. And that John Walton was his son and next heir and of full age. John Walton now sought admittance and it was granted. Fine 2d by the pledge of John Swayne.

Sum of this halmote 39s 10½d.

Sum of the two halmotes aforesaid in the charge of the greave of Ightenhill 112s 4½d

Fines for land 52s 4½d; amercements 60s.

Approved and charged in the 13th year of Queen Elizabeth.

Halmote of the manor of Tottington held at Holcome, Tuesday, 6th February 13 Elizabeth I [1570/1] before John Towneley, esq., chief steward there.

Inquisition taken there for the Queen to make enquiry upon the oaths of Lawrence Rawstorne, gent., Francis Garside, gent., Charles Nuttal, Richard Romesbothome, Edmund Lawe, Thomas Wood, Richard Boithe, Ralph Hauworth, Henry Cowop, senior, John Holte, Thomas Nuttall, William Brook, Thurstan Hamer, John Cowopp and Richard Smethurste.

Edward, Lord Derby, judge of Bury; the heir of Richard Assheton, esq., judge of Myddleton; the heir of Robert Langley, knight, judge of Alcrington, and Edmund Assheton, esq., judge of Chatterton and Foxdenton, appeared in court by their attornies.

The constables of Bury, Myddleton, Alcrington and Chatt'ton and Foxde'ton appeared in court.

Richard Boithe was elected constable [*crossed out*] greave of Tottington; Lawrence Rawstorne, gent., and John Holte were elected affeerors; Thomas Nuttall and Thurstan Hamer were elected appraisers; Henry Cowoop and Edmund Lawe were elected fence lookers; Thomas Wood and John Cowoop were elected moss lookers; Francis Garside and Richard Romesbothome were elected pounders; and Richard Rawstorne and William Broke were elected ale tasters.

James Holte (6d) because he kept his fences open between his land and tenement and the common pasture called Derden and because he unlawfully harried the cattle of his neighbours and the Queen's tenants in Tottington.

James Assheworth (4d) because he kept an illegal way in Etenfeilde Lane.

The said James (4d) because he got turfs in Tottington and carried them out of the manor.

Amercements 14d.

Henry Holte, greave of Tottington, surrendered one close of land called Withen Wall containing 3 acres of land in Tottington with its appurtenances and part of land in Alden, which Christopher Boithe delivered to him, to Richard Rawstorne and his assigns for the life of the said Christopher Bothe. Admittance sought and granted. Fine 12d by the pledge of John Grenehaulghe.

Henry Holte, greave of Tottington, surrendered one close of land called Boithecrofte containing 2 acres of land in Tottington with its appurtenances and part of land in Alden, which Christopher Boithe delivered to him, to Nicholas Wheywall and his assigns for the life of the said Christopher Bothe. Admittance sought and granted. Fine 8d by the pledge of John Grenehaulghe.

Henry Holt, greave of Tottington, surrendered one close called Rysshieacre containing 2 acres of land in Tottington with its appurtenances and part of land in Alden, which Christopher Boith delivered to him, to Matilda Barlawe, widow, and her assigns for the life of the said Christopher Boith. Admittance sought and granted. Fine 8d by the pledge of John Grenehaulghe.

John Holte surrendered one house and 1 rood of land in le Birtcheheye with common of pasture and appurtenances in Tottington and its part of land in Alden, to Ralph Lummas and his assigns for forty-nine years from the date of this halmote. Admittance sought and granted. Fine 1d by the pledge of John Anysworth.

Fee of Tottington

Inquisition taken there to make enquiry upon the oaths Ellis Romesbothome, Thomas Key, Thomas Roithewell, Ralph Aspinall, Richard Kirkema', Lamuel Openshawe, Adam Hulton, Giles Bradley, Henry Thomsone, William Ogden, Thomas Neilde, Edward Smethurste, John Whitacar and John Hill.

Edmund Nuttall (2s) because he made an affray on Richard Gryme.
Amercements 2s.

Greave

[*Presumably the following surrender should have been enrolled before the entry for the Fee of Tottington.*]

Edward, Earl of Derbei, surrendered by Lawrence Rawstorne, gent., one cottage and 1 acre of land adjacent to the east side of a certain chapel in Tottington called Holcome Chappell with common of pasture and appurtenances in Tottington and its part of land in Alden, to Henry Nuttall and Mary, his wife, and their assigns for their lives. Admittance sought and granted. An annual rent of 12d was payable to Lord Derby. Fine 4d by the pledge of John Holt.

Sum of this halmote 5s 11d.

[*Membrane 9d*]

Halmote of the manor of Tottington held at Holcome, Tuesday, 8th May 13 Elizabeth I [1571] before John Towneley, esq., chief steward there.

Inquisition taken there for the Queen to make enquiry upon the oaths of John Holt, Richard Romesbothome, Thomas Grenehaulgh, Thomas Nuttowe, Thomas Woode, Ralph Bridge, William Brok, Henry Cowoope, Thurstan Hamer, Richard Roithwell, James Assheworth, Charles Nuttowe, Richard Nuttowe and Richard Schoefeild.

Edward, Earl of Derbei, judge of Burye; the heir of Richard Assheton, judge of Myddleton; the heir of Robert Langley, knight, judge of Alcrington; and Edmund

Assheton, judge of Chatt'ton and Foxdenton appeared in court by their attornies.

The constables of Burye, Middleton, Alcrington and Chatt'ton and Foxdenton appeared in court.

The third part of two messuages and 11 acres with common of pasture and appurtenances in Tottington and their part of land in Alden came into the Queen's hands by the death of John Leyland. Thomas Leyland was his son and next heir and aged about four years. Edmund Barlowe and Geoffrey Lumasse forbade fine as they had the premises for a certain term of years. Thomas Leyland found pledge William Broke to answer the forbid and was then admitted. Fine 3s 8d by the pledge aforesaid.

John Broke (2d) because he dug pits and holes in the common pasture of Tottington.

Christopher Key (2d) did likewise.

Hamlet Law (2d) because he broke the Queen's soil and ground upon the common pasture of Tottington and got stones there.

George Nuttawe (2d) and James Holme (2d) did likewise.

Amercements 8d.[*sic*]

One messuage, other buildings and 72 acres of land with common of pasture and appurtenances in Tottington and their part of land in Alden came into the Queen's hands by the death of Ralph Holden, esq. Thomas Holden was his kinsman and next heir and aged about eighteen years. Admittance sought. Thomas Holden, clerk, forbade fine by the right of his inheritance. Isabel Holden, widow, forbade fine for her dower. Oliver Holden, John Holden, Gilbert Holden, Richard Holden, Thomas Kenyon, Joan, wife of one Robert Heighe, and Gilbert Heighe forbade fine as they had the property for certain terms of years. The said Thomas Holden, son of Gilbert Holden, found pledges Thomas Grenehaulgh, esq., and Francis Garsyde, gent., to answer the forbids and was then admitted. Fine 24s by the pledges aforesaid.

Ralph Holte of Edons surrendered by Richard Boithe, greave of Tottington, one messuage, other buildings and 2½ acres of land called Edons with common of pasture and appurtenances in Tottington and their part of land in Alden, to Thomas Warberton of Redleze and John Romesbothome of Romesbothome and their heirs as feofees according to the intent. Admittance sought and granted. Fine 10d by the pledge of Charles Nuttowe.

The intent was that the feofees were to be seised of the property to the use of the said Ralph Holte and his heirs for ever. Provided always that if he, his heirs, executors or assigns did not pay £9 to Thomas Warberton of Okenheadwood or his executors or assigns at the feast of St. Michael the Archangel [29th September] 1580 (according to the meaning of one obligation), then the feofees were to be seised to the use of Edward, son and heir of Lawrence Rawstorne, and Richard, son and heir of Richard Rawstorne, and their assigns for ever.

Henry Holt, greave of Tottington, surrendered half of one messuage, other buildings and 17 acres of land with common of pasture and appurtenances in Tottington and their part of land in Alden, which Roger Holt delivered to him, to Charles Nuttowe and Arthur Key and their heirs as feofees according to the intent. Admittance sought and granted. Fine 5s 8d by the pledge of Thomas Grenehaulghe.

The intent was that the feofees were to be seised of the property to the use of Ellen, lately wife of Roger Key, deceased, and her heirs for ever. Provided always that if the said Roger Holte, his executors or assigns paid £20 to the said Ellen, her executors or assigns at or before the feast of St. Philip and St. James next [1st May], then the feofees were to be seised to the use of the said Roger Holte and his heirs for ever.

[Membrane 10]

Afterwards, Charles Nuttowe and Arthur Keye, feofees, (at the request of the said Ellen Keye, widow) surrendered the property to Roger Holt and his heirs for ever. Admittance sought and granted. Fine 5s 8d by the pledge of Richard Boithe.

Roger Holte surrendered the fourth part of one messuage and the fourth part of 37 acres 3 roods of land with common of pasture and appurtenances in Tottington and their part of land in Alden, to Henry Holte and John Asmole and their heirs as feofees according to the intent. Admittance sought and granted. Fine 2s 6d by the pledge of John Grenehaulghe.

The intent was that the feofees were to be seised of the property to the use of Robert, son of the said Roger Holte, and Grace Grenehaulgh for their lives. And after their deaths to the use of their lawfully begotten heirs and in default of such issue to the right heirs of the said Roger Holte for ever.

Fee of Tottington
Inquisition taken there for the Queen to make enquiry upon the oaths of Roger Ogden, Thomas Key, Edmund Fenton, Lawrence Fletcher, Richard Holte, Thomas Lyvesey, Edmund Heywood, Richard Wilde, Henry Tomlinson, William Ogden, Thomas Wilde, Edward Smethurste, John Whitacar and James Buckeley.

William Bamforth (2s) because he kept an illegal way within his land and tenement leading between Rachedale and Bury.

The vill of Alcrington (2s) because they did not have 'Buttes' within the said vill. And nothing else to present because all was well.

Sum of this halmote 47s.

Sum of the two halmotes aforesaid 52s 11d
Greave; 46s 11d; fines for land 45s 1d; amercements 22d
Bailiff; 6s total of amercements.
Approved and charged in the 13th year of Queen Elizabeth.

[Membrane 10d]
[Blank]

INDEX OF NAMES

A name occurring more than once on the same page is indexed only once.

Goodshaw, John, 68
Greenacres, Richard, 1, 2, 32, 67
Greenhalgh, Bartholomew, 31
    Francis, 30, 65
    Grace, 96
    John, 31, 65, 93, 94, 96
    Thomas, 29, 30, 62, 63, 64, 94, 95, 96
Greenwood, Ambrose, 21
    John, 21, 90
    William, 21
Gregory, Charles, 11
    George, 15
    Richard, 15, 77
    Robert, 6, 19, 34, 38, 79
Grime, Alexander, 28, 87
    Charles, 87
    James, 12, 38
    John, 29
    Richard, 94
Grimshaw, John, 24, 44
    Nicholas, 79
    Percival, 38
    Richard, 24, 44

H

Habergham, Lawrence, 24, 45, 46, 55
    Richard, 24
Hall, Richard, 30
Halstead (Halstead alias Leis), Henry, 26
    Hugh, 5, 13, 14, 15, 19, 23, 25, 26,
    28, 43, 48, 84, 89, 90
    John, 22, 28, 81, 88, 89, 90, 92
    Margaret, 26
    Nicholas, 5, 46
    Oliver, 81, 88
    Richard, 5
    Robert, 28, 89
    William, 25, 26, 47, 48, 88, 89, 90
Hamer, Thurstan, 29, 30, 62, 63, 64, 93, 94
Hammond, Thomas, 68
Hancock, Elizabeth, 6
    John, 5, 6, 43, 45
    Nicholas, 5, 45, 59
    William, 43, 90, 91
Hanson (Hanson alias Bent), John, 27, 87
    William, 17, 19, 21, 41, 50, 51, 53,
    73, 74
Harger, Nicholas, 22, 88, 92
Hargreaves, Alice, 81
    Christopher, 8, 12, 14, 19, 33, 35, 38,
    51

Edward, 2, 14, 56, 69
Geoffrey, 3, 72
George, 7, 9, 11, 14, 15, 35, 36, 39,
77, 78
Henry, 2, 9, 36
Hugh, 70
James, 3, 4, 5, 57, 60, 69, 70, 72, 75,
91
Jennet, 75, 91
John, 3, 4, 5, 17, 20, 22, 24, 36, 42,
53, 56, 59, 69, 70, 71, 72, 73, 74, 75,
85, 87, 90, 91, 92
Lawrence, 69, 72
Nicholas, 22, 26, 43, 45
Richard, 6, 11, 34, 60, 75, 81
Robert, 72, 91
William, 4, 5, 46
Harrison (Heiryson), John, 1, 19, 20, 66, 85
    William, 32, 33, 68
Harrop, James, 2, 32, 33, 66, 68
    John, 2, 66, 68
Hartley (Hartley alias Byrdie), Agnes, 4, 54,
    58, 59
    Alice, 5
    Bernard (Barnard), 4, 5, 18, 51, 52,
    53, 55, 56, 58, 59, 61, 62, 70, 73
    Christopher, 2, 5, 14, 18, 42, 52, 53,
    56, 59, 70, 71, 72, 73
    Edmund, 18
    Edward, 53
    Geoffrey, 14, 18, 51, 59, 73
    Gilbert, 17, 54, 55, 73
    Henry, 4, 10, 17, 19, 23, 49, 51, 52,
    53, 56, 58, 59, 70, 71, 73
    Humphrey, 5, 70
    Isabel, 57, 61
    James, 14, 18, 19, 38, 51, 52, 56, 58,
    59, 73
    Jennet, 38
    John, 3, 4, 5, 10, 19, 49, 53, 57, 60,
    61, 63, 65, 69
    Lawrence, 5, 18, 51, 52, 56
    Margaret, 73
    Peter, 56, 59, 73
    Richard, 2, 18, 23, 51, 52, 53, 56, 59,
    69, 72, 73
    Robert, 10, 18, 19, 51, 52, 54, 55, 56,
    61, 73, 75
    Roger, 14, 18, 19, 42, 51, 52, 53, 56,
    73
    William, 6, 17, 20, 48, 49, 53, 55, 60,
    70, 87

Haslom (Hasilham), Margaret, 15
Haworth, Agnes, 16, 17
    Alexander, 42, 78
    Charles, 77
    Dionysius, 7, 8, 9, 11, 12, 15, 16, 17,
      35, 36, 38, 39, 41, 42, 76, 77, 80, 81
    Edmund, 65
    Elizabeth, 82
    Geoffrey, 29
    George, 16, 17, 42
    Henry, 15, 35, 41, 42, 51, 59, 77, 78,
      82, 85
    Isabel, 78
    James, 12, 15, 85
    Joan, 8
    John, 14, 16, 17, 35, 41, 42, 65, 77,
      82
    Nicholas, 27, 28
    Ottiwell, 42, 80
    Ralph, 10, 30, 38, 59, 62, 64, 79, 85,
      93
    Robert, 12, 35, 42, 51, 63, 76, 79
    Thomas, 78
Haydock, Evan (Owen), 28, 47, 48, 78, 88
    Simon, 78
Hayward, Richard, 79
Heald, John, 29
Heap, Henry, 6, 10, 38
    Jennet, 38
    John, 10, 11, 38, 78, 79
    Miles, 12
    Peter, 78
Hewhard see Heywood
Hey (Heigh), Gilbert, 39, 95
    Hugh, 39, 85
    Jennet, 39
    Joan, 95
    John, 22, 64, 86
    Richard, 26, 39, 76
    Robert, 11, 38, 39, 64, 79, 95
Heywood (Haywoode, Hewhard), Edmund,
    30, 63, 96
Higgin, Henry, 55
    Jennet, 43, 50
    John, 20, 22, 26, 43, 49, 50, 53, 54,
      92
Hill, Gilbert, 11, 15, 36, 78
    John, 94
Hindle, Elizabeth, 58
    Richard, 58
Hird, John, 1, 20, 32, 33
    Margaret, 32

    Nicholas, 32
    Thomas, 34
Hirste see Hurste
Hodgedene, Richard, 65
Hodgson, Robert, 91
    Thomas, 33, 68
Hodson, William, 20
Holden, Adam, 6, 7, 9, 11, 34, 37, 38, 40,
    79, 80, 85
    Gilbert, 95
    Henry, 12, 16, 35
    Isabel, 95
    James, 10
    John, 95
    Lawrence, 13, 35, 51, 80
    Nicholas, 13
    Oliver, 95
    Ralph, 6, 11, 62, 95
    Richard, 95
    Thomas, 8, 95
Hole (Hoole), Elizabeth, 81
    Giles, 81
    Miles, 15, 77
    Richard, 66, 85
Holgate, Christopher, 39
    Edmund, 73
    John, 39
Holme, James, 95
Holroyd (Hollrod), Thomas, 24
Holt, Alexander, 29, 66
    Arthur, 29
    Charles, 62
    Christopher, 63
    Edmund, 29
    Edward, 66
    Francis, 15
    Henry, 64, 65, 93, 94, 96
    Isabel, 63
    James, 93
    John, 29, 30, 41, 62, 64, 93, 94
    Peter, 64
    Ralph, 95
    Richard, 63, 96
    Robert, 96
    Roger, 96
Horrocks, John, 29
Horsfall, John, 21
Houghton, Alexander, 68
    John, 19, 24, 25, 26, 27, 42, 46, 48,
     88
    Robert, 26, 27, 43, 90
Huet, John, 55

INDEX OF PLACES

D

Danes House (Dancerhowse), 47, 48
Deadwenclough, 7, 8, 9, 12, 14, 15, 16, 35, 38, 42, 51, 78, 85, 86
Dean, 4, 27
Dearden, 93
Deep Clough (Dipe Clough) [Pendle], 59
Dunkenhalgh, 19, 84
Dunnockshaw, 78
Dysnoppe, 58
Dyveleche [Tottington], 63

E

Edenfield, 64
Edenfield Lane, 93
Edge [Colne], 19, 20
Edgend [Ightenhill], 45
Edons [Tottington], 95
Elton, 30
Emmott Lane [Colne], 20, 52
Ewood, 21, 38, 66, 79
Extwistle, 89, 90

F

Fearns [Rossendale], 15, 85, 86
Fence, 4, 57, 59, 60, 61, 71
Fernyfold [Ightenhill], 46
Fernyhalgh [Accrington], 7
Fernyside [Colne], 74, 75
Firbarne [Pendle], 58
Fletcher House [Padiham], 23
Foxdenton, 29, 30, 62, 93, 95
Friarhill, 8, 14, 39, 78, 81
Fulledge (Fullage), 23, 25, 47, 48, 89

G

Gambleside, 9, 14, 36, 38, 41, 76
Gannow, 45
Gawthorpe, 89
Goldshaw, 2, 4, 5, 17, 22, 53, 55, 56, 57, 60, 61, 69, 70, 71, 72, 73, 75, 91, 92
Goldshaw Booth, 3, 55, 70, 71
Goodshaw Booth, 35
Graystone Dole [Rossendale], 85
Greaveclough, 16, 42
Green, 24
Greenfield, 74, 75, 87
Greswell [Colne], 17
Grimehouse [Burnley], 47, 48

H

Habergham, 23, 45
Habergham Eaves, 19, 22, 23, 44, 45, 48, 87
Hagg, 21
Halcote Edge [Colne], 50
Hallton de le Hill [Craven], 25, 26
Hamstonclif [Little Marsden], 22
Haslingden, 6, 7, 9, 10, 11, 17, 34, 37, 38, 40, 42, 79, 86
Hawkshaw [Accrington], 7
Hawkshey [Ightenhill], 48
Hawkshole [Pendle], 22
Healey, 20, 23, 26, 27, 43, 48, 89, 90
Henfield, 7
Henheads, 8, 9, 14, 15, 16, 17, 35, 39, 77, 78, 80, 81, 83
Hensall, 89
Heasandford [Briercliffe], 78, 88
Hey Booth, 72
High Halstead, 28
High Hill, 3
High Ridehalgh, 89, 90
High Riley, 82, 83
High Whitaker, 90, 91
Higham, 2, 4, 5, 6, 22, 45, 56, 57, 58, 59, 69, 70
Higham Dean, 5, 57, 69
Higham Yate, 59
Hill, 22, 25, 48, 92
Hoarstones [Fence], 4
Hoddlesden, 10, 40
Holcombe, 28, 30, 62, 64, 93, 94
Hole House [Tottington], 64
Hollin Greave, 22, 25, 28, 63, 92
Hollynheigh [Colne], 21
Holme, 21, 23, 71, 91
Holmes [Bacup], 78
Holt House [Colne], 55
Horlaw Head [Rossendale], 11, 12, 40
Hulhill [Colne], 17
Huncoat, 34, 35, 40, 41, 79, 82
Hunter Holme, 24
Hurstwood, 23, 25, 26, 36

I

Ightenhill, 2, 4, 22, 26, 28, 42, 44, 45, 46, 48, 56, 57, 58, 59, 69, 70, 86, 89, 90, 92
Ightenhill Park, 23

S

Sabden, 69, 70, 71, 75, 91
Sabden Bank, 43, 91
Sabden Hey, 22
Sawreave, 44
Scarr, 32
Scolebank [Padiham], 22, 44, 66, 88, 89
Sedewast [Rossendale], 85, 86
Sedges [Rossendale], 12, 13, 37, 77
Sefton, 5
Shawclough [Rossendale], 37, 77
Shawe Hills [Rossendale], 77
Shelfeld [Colne], 53
Shipperbottom, 30
Shuttleworth, 63
Simonstone, 25, 27, 46, 91
Southfield [Colne], 21, 50
Sowclough [Rossendale], 12, 13, 37, 77, 78
Standes, 85
Stanrod (Stanrodhall) [Colne], 20, 21, 74
Stoidley, 21
Stryndes [Haslingden], 38
Swinden, 19, 54, 73, 89
Swinshaw, 78

T

Tottington, 28, 29, 30, 31, 32, 62, 63, 64, 65, 66, 93, 94, 95, 96
Towneley, 78
Trawden, 18, 20, 21, 51, 52, 53, 54, 55, 56, 59, 73, 75, 76
Tunstead, 12, 13, 14, 15, 37, 38, 52, 76, 77
Tunstead Heys [Rossendale], 76
Tyndehead Yate [Pendle], 70
Tynstead [Pendle], 57

U

Ugden *see* Ogden

V

Vyver [Colne], 18, 74

W

Walkefield [Colne], 20
Walverden, 17, 23
Water Meetings, 69
West Close, 3, 6, 56, 71, 75, 91
Westby, 55, 57
Wetehead [Rossendale], 39
Wheatley Hey Booth, 3, 23, 69, 71, 72
Whitfield [Ightenhill], 87
Whithalgh [Pendle], 61, 72
Windle House, 22, 89, 90, 92
Winewall, 18, 19, 50, 51, 52, 56, 59, 73
Wolfenden, 8, 9, 10, 11, 12, 13, 14, 15, 16, 35, 36, 37, 39, 40, 41, 42, 76, 77, 79, 80, 81, 82, 85, 86
Wolfenden Booth, 8, 9, 16, 80, 81, 85
Wood Hey, 63
Worsthorne, 28, 44
Worston, 1, 2, 19, 32, 33, 34, 66, 67, 69
Wycollar, 42, 51, 52, 56, 59, 73
Wyteheade (Wethead) [Colne], 49, 53

Y

Yate, 35
Yatefield [Ightenhill], 23, 46
Yorkshire, 25, 26, 36, 72

INDEX OF THINGS